I0469907

The Marketing Doctor's Survival Notes

A Collection of Tips, Techniques for Survival from the
Trenches of Corporate and Non-profit Marketing

DAVID POULOS

Copyright © 2013 David Poulos
All rights reserved.

ISBN: 1481103105
ISBN-13: 9781481103107

Library of Congress Control Number: 2012922398
CreateSpace Independent Publishing Platform
North Charleston, South Carolina

Acknowledgements

Edited by Edwin G. Sapp, J. D. USAF (Ret.). Dr Sapp is the chair of professional writing courses at the University of Maryland's University College

Thanks to Gregg Burrage and his crew at Rings Leighton Design for the cover design.

Special thanks to Renee Sciuto Novak for the inspiration to write this, with the alternate title "The World According to Dave."

TABLE OF CONTENTS

Introduction

The following is a collection of articles, blog posts and essays created over four years, during one of the worst economic recessions in American history. During economic contractions, recessions and other disruptions, one of the first things that American corporations and non-profits do, in knee-jerk reaction to a reduction in sales volume and revenue, is to cut expenses in order to survive. Unfortunately, one of the most often-cut 'expenses' is the marketing budget. Some of these tips were put together to bolster the spirits of those unfortunate corporate or non-profit marketers living in fear and paralysis, afraid to lose their jobs, their budget, their livelihood, because their boss or the CEO didn't grasp the simple truth that money spent on marketing activities of various kinds is not an expense, it's an investment in your business' future. Some of these tips were put together to inform and enlighten less-experienced marketers, who would otherwise have to learn things the hard way, so they might get some value from the mistakes of others who came before them. Some of them are simply a way of codifying marketing behavior in the light of common sense – everybody can 'do' marketing, right?

The elements presented here are based on over thirty years of observation, experience and understanding how to make products, brands, companies and organizations look their best to customers, serve customers better, grow and thrive. They are largely opinions, not scholarly research, although facts as presented are based on real-world situations I've encountered working in, or consulting with, real-world organizations. They should be taken at face value – it's not exactly a 'How-To' book, these are not 'unbreakable rules', there's no hidden agenda here, no subtle sub-text to be deciphered, no underlying mystery to be uncovered. It's a book of principals, guidelines, brief vignettes of experiences that might have value to those just entering the field, or those transitioning from another pocket of the profession. It's a book, perhaps not THE Book, but the principals it posits are sound and worth the time to read.

I hope you enjoy reading it, that you learn something from it, that you try to adopt some of the philosophies, some of the techniques, and absorb some of the lessons in the stories presented here.

Go forth and be successful . . .

1) Marketing Philosophy

Does Your Campaign Pass The Sniff Test?

Good Morning!
I've been working with business clients to assist them in their marketing efforts for nearly three decades, and in that time, there have been very few rules that I haven't broken, bent, or ignored altogether. There is one, however, that no matter what your industry or line of business, needs to be present somewhere in the mix - The Sniff Test.

Human beings evolved over millions of years, surviving due to an over-sized brain and an ability to use that brain power to adapt his environment to suit his needs. One of those adaptations is a facet of the primitive, limbic portion of the brain that senses danger. Things like the hair on the back of your neck standing up, or a queasy feeling in your gut, or a general uneasiness in the back of your mind that tells you there's someone in the house or that you're being watched. That's instinct, it's your subconscious processing what you see and feel and hear and smell, and putting out a primitive nervous signal that there's something your conscious brain is missing, because it's too busy working on what's coming . . . That instinct was developed to keep you alive.

That same instinct is useful in business, when reviewing partners, business arrangements, marketing strategy, new product development, and other areas where it's easy to get caught up in the hype and the hysteria, and execute strategies that do not have a strong foundation in logic and data. That is the instinct I call the "sniff test," and it's really a jaded, realistic way of looking at a worst-case scenario by stripping away all the "possibles" and "maybes" in the scenario planning, leaving just the facts.

Say the marketing manager comes to you with a campaign idea that involves the buyer or customer to follow five or six steps in order to redeem a coupon in a product offer, and when you do the math on the offer, the numbers don't really offer any advantage to the buyer after all the rebates, savings certificates and all the rest is computed. Take a step back, pretend you're in the grocery store and have two products side by side, yours and your competitor's. Now read the offer slowly and carefully, and add weight to your competitor's product for every step you have to take, in order to get the savings the coupon represents. Now subtract weight for every ten cents' worth of different in price you offer over your competitor's product. If your product price doesn't outweigh all the work needed to get it, the offer doesn't pass the sniff test. Despite how it works on paper, in the real world, it just won't smell good to the consumer. Even if it's explicitly spelled out that the savings are significant, it will send up a flag for the consumer if it's too hard to do - too many places for error to creep in, too much work, too many conditions, it will just feel like you're trying to put one over on them, and they'll pick the "safe" option - instinct at work.

Unconsciously, you use the sniff test every day, to evaluate deals, employee performance, new hires, as a lie detector in presentations or meetings - anywhere you place a value judgment not strictly based in logic. If someone asked you after one of those decisions why you went the way you did, you couldn't give a solid, logical answer, you'll likely think to yourself "it just doesn't smell right" - you just implemented the sniff test, and whatever you were evaluating didn't pass.

Can We Predict The Future?

Wouldn't it be terrific if we knew what the future held for each of us? Even if you were living just a few minutes ahead of everyone else, what fun would it be knowing what others around you didn't know. How would you use the information?

I think if I were to live ten minutes ahead and therefore seem to know the future up to ten minutes from now, I'd use it to communicate more effectively with those around me. How cool would it be if you could "know" how the person across the table would react to your next statement and have ten minutes to test it out, see the reaction, and fix it before the other person knew what had happened?

In our marketing practice, we are often asked to tell clients their future when they ask us, "how well do you think this campaign will do" or "should we hire extra people in fulfillment or customer service to ramp up to handle the response we'll get", and my response is often "it might be a good idea" - admittedly a little vague, positive, but non-committal.

I don't have a crystal ball, I don't tell fortunes, and I don't live ten minutes ahead of the rest of the world, so "I don't know" is the best answer. I do know that if you've done your homework, based your creative executions on research (both primary and secondary, internal and external), and you BELIEVE and act only on the data, then you won't go too far wrong. You might just need extra help in fulfillment of the extra orders, but it might be better to wait and see how it goes. If things explode, get a couple of temporary employees in the next day as a stopgap measure until you can hire more permanent staff for a sustained effort. If your fulfillment set up is designed correctly, you should be able to make up for a one-or two-day lag in a few hours or an extra shift overnight, in order to live up to your shipping promise. Of course, all that is predicated on that fulfillment staff having product available to work with.

As you do more campaigns, and you get a sense for whether each is going to create a bump in sales and fulfillment requests, you'll be able to gauge better your staffing and product resource needs. Having put together over 100 campaigns in the last two decades, I can tell you that they are all different, have different goals, different levels of what is considered a success, and we still get surprised by the positive sales response clients receive - surprised in a good way.

Next time you're contemplating embarking on a marketing campaign, ask yourself what's the worst that could happen - it doesn't move the needle on sales, right? What's the best that can happen? You're swamped with orders and have to scramble to catch up. Not really a bad problem to have, especially under difficult economic circumstances. Worst-case scenario, by learning what doesn't work with your customers, you can avoid doing something similar in the future, and you've learned something concrete and useful about your customers - not a bad way to spend a little money on primary research . . .

Teamwork Pays Off

One especially severe winter, our family had been paying the price for Mother Nature's wrath, including over 4' of snow, by replacing the 28-year-old roof on our house. We talked to roofers and selected one with a large number of crews and manpower to draw from, and after checking out some of their work, set up a contract based on an agreed-to price, and waited for the crew to arrive. A week or so later, the project manager called and said we'd be receiving a delivery of our shingles the next day, and that the job would be done in one day. We were amazed, as the roof is rather large and complicated as roofs go, lots of valleys and it's a hip roof, so there's lots of guttering and ridge cap and such - a big job for most crews.

The day came, and at an early hour, four trucks pulled into the driveway and disgorged over a dozen workers, including a huge flatbed delivery truck with a remote operated hydraulic crane. They proceeded to unload their gear, get their materials in place and set to work, with very little conversation or communication of any kind. Like a well-oiled machine, they each knew their role and carried it out at the right time in the right order, and low and behold, within 24 hours of their starting time, the job was completed, just a few moments shy of a thunderstorm.

Think how effective your marketing team is when faced with a challenge of this magnitude, how they are given direction, how they work together, how much they accomplish in a compressed time frame. To most office-based teams, the level of teamwork and coordination evidenced by these roofers is not only impossible, but alien to their nature. Not one of these workers told the others, "no, it's your job, I'll only handle this" or "I'm on a break, you do it" or pointed any fingers at the others when there was a discrepancy - they just worked quietly and competently alongside one another, and got the job done, so they could go home. They were quiet, respectful of not only us and our property but of each other. And these were not highly paid, well-read educated executives, they were hourly laborers.

There is great value in knowing your job thoroughly, understanding your role in the organization, taking responsibility for yourself and your actions, and doing a job well. Working in a team that functions smoothly involves all of this and more. Some of the responsibility for the team's success falls to the leader, or manager, of the team. Clearly this team had been trained, and supervised carefully until they worked together well, but that wasn't all of it. Part of their success lies in believing in a common purpose - "us against the mountain" mentality, rising to the occasion to meet a common challenge. The sense of personal accomplishment is shared by all, and they can retire at the end of the day knowing they accomplished a job well done. In return, they received a steady stream of work, a reasonable pay, and the admiration of their customers and colleagues alike for a tough task accomplished.

If only some of our leaders and top executives in the financial community took some of those values to heart, we'd all be in a better place right now. The leaders failed the team and the public in those cases, and education or compensation for the job didn't have anything to do with it.

Next time you're going to initiate a new marketing campaign, pull your team together for a kick-off meeting and try and instill those same values those roofers showed in your team. It's tougher than it sounds . . .

Change Is Good . . .

Change generally is good, for a majority of the people, a majority of the time. However fear of the unknown often retards the advance of change, and after a few surprises, it's easy to become change-averse and fearful of the outcome of any change in our lives.

Many people have experienced a change in the last couple of years that can be the most disruptive of nearly all events in our lives - the loss of a job. This has been ranked up there with a death in the family in terms of negative feelings, depressive influence, and life interruption. Those whose livelihoods and lifestyle was most dependent upon that weekly income are those most profoundly affected, and those who were the least prepared, i.e. having no savings or cushion, were the ones that felt the pinch most severely. Those that embraced the change, reassessed their situation in a realistic, fearless way, were able to use their strengths, and send their lives in a new, positive direction. Many started their own businesses, gaining control over their income, their lives and their schedule. Some found new careers through retraining, additional education or volunteering through other organizations that lead to a new position. Change managed and channeled is change for the better; activity takes away the fear and returns you to a position of control.

In business, change must be managed carefully through frequent, relevant communication, strong leadership, and transparent planning. The less employees fear, the more likely they are to embrace the new order and get with the program in a positive way. The economy has forced changes on virtually every business out there, and some have managed those changes with the least damage to employees and their bottom line, and come out stronger at the other end as a result. Other have employed more drastic slash-and-burn tactics, and are now hunting for talent, hurting for cash, and have lost market share to their competitors who were ready to gear up for growth.

Marketing is often the promoter and enactor, a catalyst for change - how our company looks to the world affects how we work internally, which drives process change. New marketing programs bring changes in business processes, like customer service, order fulfillment, purchasing, invoicing, vendor selection, even physical plant management and HR. That kind of broad ranging change can bring some heat to the marketing department, but if managed correctly, can lead to a stronger, more visible, more progressive company in the long-run.

Communicate often, make it relevant, tell workers what's going to be coming down the pike, give them time to process and absorb it, react to it, vent about it, and accept and embrace it - once people get comfortable with the new order, they'll wonder how they did things any other way . . .

The Devil's In the Details

Sometimes it's the little things that make a difference in the effectiveness of your marketing campaign. I'm not talking about typos, color shifts, production problems etc. Those can be controlled and at some point there are enough eyes on the material that they will likely be found and corrected before too much damage is done, at least in the old days, before instant campaigns online became possible.

Today it's a little different, in that with speed comes a greater margin for error, often born of impatience. Get it out there; get it out there, no matter what the cost in accuracy or efficacy. The number of eyes on the materials has been greatly reduced, as the influence and assistance of outside vendors, editors, production artists, printers, mail shop workers, shippers, packagers, truck drivers, etc. have been greatly reduced or eliminated. You can now "do it all yourself" and when the mistakes surface, you have only yourself to blame.

The little things I'm talking about are those small details in the offer, those small production details like proportion and size relationships, and typography, and color selection, and all the other little elements that make up a successful mail campaign. Promotion codes that work, addresses that are postal-validated or permit numbers that are correct, phone numbers and web addresses that are accurate and that function correctly. And more importantly, concepts that actually sell the right product! You might think I'm exaggerating or embellishing for effect, but I've seen marketing pieces that appear to sell the wrong product. I mean wrong compared to the intent of the sponsoring organization. If you are a large manufacturer, and your product contains a licensed product or another branded ingredient under a specific arrangement, (like laundry detergent with Fabreeze), you can stop reading here. That's not what I mean.

The essential details I'm referring to emerge when the marketing team gets so involved in the details required to produce the piece, that nobody has taken a step back and asked the critical question "What are we selling here?" Those little elements I mentioned above can indeed have a huge impact on the outcome of the campaign (think what could happen if you've got four or five sponsors or tests and each has a different promo code, and somehow the codes get shifted mid-way or they all lead the same place and don't differentiate - your metrics are shot, you have no idea how to assign revenue, and your test is inconclusive and invalid - not a good day to be working in the marketing department). But if your focus of the campaign is off, you've fundamentally misdirected the audience's attention, diluted the impact of your campaign, and wasted potentially a lot of money. When reading the copy, those first clues that the focus has shifted will likely emerge. If you get to the end of reading the raw copy, no images, no production, just words on paper, and you don't feel motivated to find out how to get hold of that product, start over.

Laser-like focus is required for maximum results. Each word, phrase, image, element or choice should be selected and added because it enhances the power of the message, clarifies the intent of the piece, or aids functionality for the end-user to facilitate a sale. Editing is a subtractive technology. Good editors take the mass of information presented in the first or second draft, and selectively remove anything that doesn't force the sale forward. What's left should be crystal clear, high-impact, high-return marketing madness that drives sales through the roof.

Once that's achieved, test it, and mail, mail, mail! If you've thought it all through thoroughly, tracked all the leads, attended to every detail, checked every phone number, web address, promo code and list parameter, success is inevitable.

The Devil's in the details, so, bold marketers, go forth and dance with the devil, knowing that solid preparation, pin-point focus, and data-driven logic are the weapons that help you control the dance!

When It Comes To Ads, Trust . . . But Verify

One of a marketer's biggest challenges is creating trust with a new audience. If a sector of your potential customer base has never heard of you, or you're breaking into a new market in which you have no previous exposure or installed base, you need to create trust with that new audience immediately.

Unfortunately, some more unscrupulous marketers using techniques that one could call questionably ethical at best, have raised the trust bar for consumers, making our job more difficult. The days when you could say practically anything on TV or radio or in print, and as long as you said it often enough, people would come to believe it, are long gone. Even politicians are discovering this to be so. The buying public has many more sources of information available to them, and many more ways to verify the information you're presenting, including speedier access to friends and advisers, websites with reviews, and more. That makes it more difficult to present information in anything but an accurate light. It also means that if you do succeed in bamboozling the public with less-than-honest product claims, that fact, once revealed, will travel faster than ever before, and word will spread at a phenomenal rate about the deceptive practices.

This means that as marketers, we have to dig deeper into the creativity well, work harder at crafting that real offer, work smarter at getting people's attention, draw down on more ways to present different benefits in an appealing way to a more wary consumer. It's not enough to just say it's "better," you have to explain why . . .

For successful marketers, that means a high level of speed and adaptability, a higher level of selectivity in media choices, and a better understanding of the chosen audience, both psychologically and behaviorally. And, now more than ever, reputation is your most valuable asset.

Advertisers go to great lengths to make their offers sound as appealing as possible, to show their products in their most flattering light - and sometimes they go too far. If you hear a claim regarding a product or company that sounds too good to be true, it's still a good bet that it shouldn't be trusted. As our once-fearless leader Ronald Reagan noted, when dealing with the unknown, "Trust . . . but verify"!

Sometimes the Question is More Important than the Answer . . .

There are times in a marketer's career when asking the right question spurs the next great idea that turns into a campaign that turns the corner on profitability and launches a whole new direction for the company or the product.

Having the curiosity and the courage to ask that question - although to you it might seem obvious, so obvious in fact that you're sure someone else must have thought of it, analyzed the result and discarded it as unworkable - is what makes marketers good. How many times have you been in a meeting and another employee asks a seemingly innocent question, and suddenly the room is on fire with ideas, and more importantly, positive feelings and agreement to trying the idea immediately. Have you kicked yourself for not asking the same thing? Why didn't you - because you thought it was too obvious. It was obvious to you, because that's the way you were trained to think - but most of the other people in the room were not trained that way, and that's what makes you special! You would never have suspected that the obvious might be the best answer, but most others find it miraculous – it s a common experience among marketers, so get used to it.

Think it through quickly, end to end, and go ahead and bring up the obvious - you'll be surprised at the reaction you'll get. Curiosity and courage linked together will get you a long way in marketing. A famous marketer I know is fond of saying that there are no bad ideas, just those that don't work under the current circumstances. His approach is to try almost anything that appears viable, and if six out of ten of them fly, he's a winner! Indeed the margin on a good idea is pretty high, so it doesn't take much for a good idea to bring in far more than all the bad ones waste. Remember the old campaign, "Try it, you'll like it"? Not a bad mantra in these tough times. Businesses are desperate for good paying customers, and ideas that will attract them are in short supply.

Step up, state your idea, and let the chips fall - you'll likely be applauded and the chips fall your way - if not, at least you put something viable forward, and if it doesn't work now, circumstances will forever change and it might work at some other time.

Marketing Leadership Means Asking the Right Questions

Ever wonder how market-leading companies got that way? Ever wonder who lead the way and how they knew to veer in the direction they did? My associates and I at Granite Partners reviewed hundreds of business cases, and we've determined that there are some key decisions that top marketing executives make in common with market leadership, the result of which is moving that company to the next level.

5) **Select Partners Carefully.** Ask yourself this question: Would I want to do business with this company regardless if I made a profit or not? If the answer is no, then it's probably not a good fit. For a partnership to work, both sides have to support the mission equally and enthusiastically. If you don't enjoy your interactions with the partner and they're not tremendously fruitful, cut your losses and dissolve it before things get bad.

4) **Know When To Call it A Day.** Ask yourself: Is this effort as effective as it was the week it started? If the answer is no, is it fatiguing and lagging due to lack of support, saturation, market shift or getting stale? It may be you've reached the point of diminishing returns, and the Return on Investment of continuing it is no longer viable. If that's the case, you're throwing money away, just pull the plug and initiate another effort. Clinging to a failing program costs you more than you imagine in lost opportunity, time, and its negative effect on your audience, staff and company morale has a measurable value.

3) **Have a Purpose.** Ask yourself: Why exactly are we doing this again? If the answer resembles something like "we did it last year," or "our competitors tried it," or "The Boss wants it that way," than it might be time to rethink the effort from the beginning. Legacy programs whose rationales have changed due to altered circumstances can be doing damage to your brand, losing you money, and wasting time. If the purpose no longer exists, don't do it!

2) **Are We Winning, and If Not, Why Not?** One thing most market leading companies use as a mantra is that they have to be in the top one or two positions in each market they compete in or changes need made. They feel a need to lead, and they do everything in their power to lead their particular category for every product or service they offer. A quick analysis of the leader will tell

you what you're doing wrong, and you have to make a decision whether to fix it or bail out. The Cost/Benefit analysis should be performed regularly, and an honest market scan quarterly.

1) **Where Do We Go From Here?** Market leaders don't often have to ask this question, because they think eight or nine moves ahead and plan strategically each move and have three contingencies based on research and market intelligence. They ask "where do we go" long before they get there! Draw the roadmap before you leave the barn, leave room to be flexible to respond to unforeseen challenges, and stay the course, and you'll be surprised how far you'll go. The control and discipline it requires to do this is what separates the men from the boys, but you can bet that market leading companies spend more time planning than executing, and spend significant time asking "What if?"

If your company wants to be a leader in their market, it comes down to asking the right questions, and probing until you get an answer that satisfies your needs. Keep digging . . .

Self Promotion Is Not a Crime

A lot of business start-up executives I encounter in my practice have an odd feeling about marketing. They seem to think that promoting themselves is somehow unseemly or impolite, simply not done. I can only thank my stars that this isn't the case, or I'd be out of a job! Self-promotion of your business is vital to its growth and continued viability. So where did the guilt come from?

I think it comes from the image of a blowhard, always talking about himself and exaggerating his prowess and bragging about how he is the biggest, best, whatever he does. We've seen them, we know of them, and we try to avoid them. But there is a distinct difference between promoting your business endeavor and bragging about its success. Done properly, self-promotion allows you to get the word out often enough, and generate enough business that your satisfied clients will do the bragging for you, so you don't have to.

Small or especially start-up businesses need to promote their existence rather heavily, and it comes more naturally to some entrepreneurs than others. Most I've met are extremely passionate about their business and very proud of their accomplishments, and rightly so. For those to whom this is a natural occurrence, they not only make it look easy, but have come to a point where it can be very subtle and low key and still be effective. That's the mark of a master, and, admittedly, few reach that level. Fortunately, some come to the realization early that this is not their forte, and they hire someone to do it for them - they're called clients at that point, and bless them all!

To be a small business owner, one thing it's difficult to be and still be successful is shy. You have to get it out there and let the public know you're there, and by doing it a few at a time, you might not ever reach critical mass needed to make it a viable business. So a strong marketing strategy, including some form of outreach promotion and advertising is usually in order. Often it's something simple, a small ad, even a classified ad is a start. Maybe send a postcard to the local area, or a short letter to the neighboring zip codes. Maybe it's a little league soccer or baseball sponsorship. But at the heart of it, it's the business owner's personality coming through, selling hard and showing that passion for their business that makes it all work.

If you've started a business in the wake of a layoff or change of life status due to the recent recession, you're in good company. SBA is reporting a record number of applications for funding and loans, and services that support small business start-ups like insurance, permits, licensing and other things are having a good year. You're off and running, congratulations! Now it's time to turn to marketing to make that little kernel of an idea grow and flourish. If you haven't done so already, decide how much you want to spend, and start saving now to fill that budget line. There is no hard and fast rule for how much to set aside. Some businesses spend over 20% of their gross income on marketing expenses, some as little as .5% - it depends on how you spend it, and what your goals are. The important thing is to get started, do something, make it happen, so the results can start working for you!

Don't be shy about self-promotion, it's not a crime, but if you just can't bring yourself to tell everyone about your new endeavor, hire someone to do it for you - it's the best money you'll ever spend.

If You Can't Measure It, It's Not a Goal

Almost every strategic planning session I've ever directed or participated in has included a section on setting goals and objectives – after all, if you don't know where you're going, you'll have a very hard time getting there. But the component that doesn't get examined as closely in that section is, "how are we going to measure this so we can gauge our success?" How else will you know if you've achieved the goal if you can't measure it? Seems simple and obvious, but I've seen countless "goals" that read like gift cards – "Increase Quality of Customer Service to Help Our Customers Better" – YUK!

Goals and objectives, whether as part of a strategic plan, part of a performance appraisal, or just a personal wish list, should fulfill three requirements:

Measurable, Timely, Valuable

Measurability is a key to making goals work. The critical element that should be at the heart of goals that will be used to drive revenue or change is specificity. Statements that say you're going to "increase" something should be further specified by "How much" and "compared to 'what'". Without those two additional elements, the value of the goal recedes and dilutes to the point of being worthless, and is almost guaranteed not to "increase" anything except wasted time.

The template should be something like: "Increase net sponsorship revenue by 25% by the end of the year compared to 2011's total" – specific, specific, measurable – a real goal.

Timeliness is next to Godliness. If you don't have a time limit on goals to not only close off the review process but to also provide some urgency, you've lost a lot of the power inherent in goal-setting. Saying you're going to accomplish something without saying "by when" is akin to lying to yourself, and will likely achieve the same result. Not only don't you know when to test your success at achieving the goal, but there's no real reason to even get started, because you don't have a deadline. There's no direction or stated purpose when the finish line in time isn't a goal unto itself. Procrastination will lead the day under those circumstances, and the goal will never really be reached in time to do anyone else any good.

The template should be: "Hire three new, experienced exhibit sales representatives and have them indoctrinated and trained by the end of the second quarter." Six months to find, hire, train and turn out three experienced space sales people is a laudable, reachable but urgent goal, one that contributes directly to the benefit of the organization – higher sales.

Valuable might seem to be an attribute that flies in the face of the specificity and granularity of the other two elements discussed here, but it's central to the goal setting process. If the goal you're setting doesn't benefit the organization as a whole, or isn't tied to something that is seen as an improvement, then its value is questionable, and with resources as scarce as they seem to be, waste should be a four-letter word for most non-profits. Certainly specificity adds strength to the value of the goal, but overall, the goal itself must be seen by members, staff, executives, Board and vendors as laudable, authentic, and meaningful. Saying you're going to "increase outreach efforts to build international goodwill for the organization" probably sounds like it would be easy to accomplish and gain almost universal acceptance. We're a society of consensus, and this one will almost always gain consensus among "right" thinking members. But let's examine it a bit more closely and see if we can make it really work for the organization as a whole.

The first red flag should be the word "effort," as it implies that you're going to try. Goals aren't about trying, they're about succeeding. No ribbon for 9th place, no medal for trying, not in business, not for non-profits. The second red flag is the amorphous term "international goodwill". Does this mean that Mexico as a whole will like your association? That Brussels will embrace your organization if you send some direct mail to potential members there? If you're trying to open new markets for your members to sell products or services to, just say that – no shame there. If you're going to expand the organization's scope to include members from other countries, that's a laudable goal, but it involves much more specificity to determine how to approach it and more importantly, why it's valuable to the organization (and to the new international confederates). The value in this goal is hidden, but if rewritten to uncover it, it becomes much more transparent and shows forethought and vision.

This is where the "strategic" part of strategic planning comes in. Does accepting international members benefit the existing membership as a whole, does it increase opportunity for those members to succeed, does it provide a direct benefit to the membership at large, or does it simply increase the size of the organization, providing staff jobs and some incremental revenue (and usually high-cost revenue as well)? If you serve a group of manufacturers in a mature, saturated, domestic market, then opening up opportunities on an international basis has tremendous value to members, and can be written as: "Open up seven non-domestic market opportunities for US-based members to supplant 10% of the domestic sales by members by the end of 2012". If those circumstances don't mirror your organization, then some serious thinking needs to go behind a goal to broaden the scope of the organization on an international basis. But, whatever your goal, it should be viewed through the lens of enhancing or benefitting the membership of the organization in total.

Give Your Goals Power

Goal-setting is a vital, critical part of any strategic planning exercise. If the goals are formulated properly, using input from all to be constrained by them, whose performance will be gauged by reaching them, they will have a much better chance of being achieved. If the goals are not specific, measurable, timely and valuable, with each missing element the chance of success degrades by over 25%, based on our own informal studies involving over 40 different non-profit organizations over 10 years.

The difference between "*increase non-dues revenue*" and "*increase non-dues revenue by 20%*" is 25% more powerful. Add timeliness – "*increase non-dues revenue by 20% by the end of 2012*" and add another 25% to the power level of that goal. Take the next step, "*increase non-dues revenue by 20% by the end of 2012, to earn sufficient funding to expand our educational foundation library*" hits a homerun and is as powerful as you can get, in terms of formulating a real goal with a specific, measurable, timely and valuable outcome. And, it has the added element of consequence – if you don't reach the goal, something else will be negatively affected. If whatever tactics you formulate to achieve the goal are too slow getting started, if they don't have the funding or the muscle required to get to the end, if they aren't seen as sufficiently valuable to earn the support of members and staff, then you won't be able to expand the library and serve members as a resource. This goal shows vision, forethought, specificity, measurability, timeliness and value, and will very likely be embraced by all stakeholders and achieved – I'd apply for the librarian's job right now, based on how well that's written!

By crafting solid, measurable goals for your organization, you present a very desirable carrot for your members and staff to work toward. By giving them a trustworthy, reliable and solid way to measure their success, one that isn't capricious or arbitrary, you provide the support and solidity they need to dig in and accomplish what the organization needs. Having a goal, working toward it and seeing the end in sight, and achieving it are very satisfying activities, and are at the root of why people join companies or are members of organizations to begin with. The feeling of "all oars in the water, rowing the same direction" is a very powerful motivator, and is extremely fulfilling to both members and staff. In reality, nothing succeeds like success, but if you can't measure it, if you can't gauge it against a benchmark, if you can't see progress, then that success is diluted and loses its power to motivate and to achieve in other endeavors.

Empower your staff, volunteers and members to move the needle forward. Set goals that make sense, that are transparent, that are reasonable, that are measurable, timely and valuable to the organization, and you increase your chances of achieving them multifold. As a byproduct, you will likely also find improvements in staff morale, in quality and volume of input from staff, volunteers, members and Board, and your membership will grow as a result. Not a bad outcome for taking a few extra minutes to edit and drive the language by which your organization will judge its success.

The Illusion of Control

I think we can agree that most top marketing professionals are what used to be called a "Type A" personality - high speed, high motivation, attention to detail, internally driven, goal oriented, with a strong need for control. Sound about right? If so, you're likely in the right role if you're a marketer, but are all of these traits actually helping you succeed? Sometimes less is more, and as a species, most of us labor under the misconception that we can control more than we really can.

That control issue can lead to problems. We can plan for just about any scenario, we can be prepared for the worst outcome, we can remove or stabilize as many variables as possible, but there is always a large element of the unknown involved in our work. That's not to say that we can give up responsibility for the outcome of any of it, but there is only so much we can control about the results of our efforts. We can't go to people's homes and force them to buy what we have to offer at gunpoint. We can only use history, research, or self-proclamation to divine the likelihood of each one buying a product, lump them all together, and put forth our best pitch based on common characteristics among the group.

We can test, but we can't control. Test results, be it focus group, direct response test, concept survey, or other method, can only give us a snapshot of the most obvious feelings and actions of the given group at that moment. If you got the same group together again the following month, you might get different results to the same test, based on circumstances beyond our, and their, control. All you can really do is play to the odds, decrease your chances of missing as much as you're able, and hope to catch potential buyers under favorable circumstances. That's not control.

On a larger scale, our lives contain the illusion of control as well. Anyone who's planned an outdoor wedding knows, you can't control everything. You can have the best vendors, the most elegant choices, the best caterer and decorator and a force-of-nature coordinator, and none of that makes up for the fact that it could rain buckets that day. You can increase your odds by considering timing, location, and site protection, but those are not control tools, just contingency planning - it's still raining, you just made it tolerable for the guests by ordering a tent.

That's not to say that such events don't have a cause somewhere that can be eliminated, deferred or altered - the Butterfly Effect is a theoretical conceptual diagram designed to show the rippling and far-reaching impact of actions in a closed system that highlights this - but at the end of the chain it is simply a set of unalterable circumstances.

Lack of control can cause us to make errors - lack of recognition of loss of control can lead to disaster. Take a direct marketing test grid. We can't control those buyers, but we can test that group of uncontrollable people's preferences as a group, and control for wide differences within the group. When we read the test results, there may be a set of data that appears inconsistent with what we know in history, with what we *feel*, with what we "think" we know. That data may be discounted as an anomaly, an aberration, some irrelevant variable that isn't affecting the overall program. But what if that piece of data, when expanded upon and tested further by itself, is critical to a strong response - that the audience needs that portion of the mailing needs to be there as a catalyst to response, and by ignoring it, we negatively affect response to a great degree going forward? Our own sense of control has effectively overwhelmed the data in front of us and reduced our effectiveness and our impact on profits with that mailing mistake.

We can't control everything, but we can control how we react to things. If your first reaction when faced with an uncontrolled situation is to hide or ignore it, or worse, try to control the uncontrollable, failure is a likely outcome. As marketers we would be better served by our flexibility, our ability to "roll with it" in our reaction to the situation, to make the best of what might be a less than desirable outcome. Plan for the worst, hope for the best, be ready for anything.

10 Things Marketers Can Do To Help Them Succeed

I wanted to give readers some forward thinking, rather than reviewing the prior events - we all know what happened, and we can't change it anyway. So, here's a few basic things to keep in mind as you move forward:

10) **A "Market" Never Bought Anything** - *people* buy things and services and ideas. When you think about or talk about your "Target Market" keep in mind that a market is actually a group of people, with ideas, moods and feelings of their own. If you can conjure up a visual image of a representative of that group, it can help focus your ideas and your copy.

9) **Its the List, Stupid!** All the creative design, top quality printing, conscientious mail services or hot offer in your direct marketing fails miserably in the wake of a bad list. Do your homework; check all the possible angles, find lists that make sense, that are fresh and accurate, and that have a recognizable reason to buy your product.

8) **Sheep Get Slaughtered.** If you're trying a new technique, a new media, a new idea or trend that's being touted as the next big thing, ask yourself "How does this help me reach my stated goals, and how will I measure its impact?" If you can't answer those honestly, you really don't have a good reason for doing whatever it is. Just because a competitor is doing it, or *"everyone's"* doing it, doesn't make it right for you.

7) **Be True To Your Brand. Period.** When you get ready to launch a new campaign, or start a new service, dust off your brand characteristics inventory (you have one of those, right?) and review those traits, and see how well your new idea matches up or illustrates those attributes. If you miss more than 25% of them, rethink the idea. You'll do more damage putting out off-brand stuff than you can make up in incoming revenue or awareness.

6) **Test, Test, Test** - You can't do enough research, you can't know enough about your customers, but their buying behavior in a real situation tells the strongest tale. Test as many variables in your mail campaign as you can, and trust the response data. When it comes time to review your results, the data will back you up a lot better than your "gut."

5) **The Harder You Work, The Luckier You'll Get** - Ideas are like those tempera paints you used in grade school - the more you throw at the wall, the more color you get to stick. Keep churning out ideas and executing them as best you can with your time constraints and budget, and while following the guidelines out lined in this section - if you throw out ten ideas and three of them bomb, that means the other seven were good enough and made up for the three duds. You win.

4) **Strive for "Works Well With Others" comments** - the more people you involve and get ideas from, the better those ideas will become. It spreads the workload, spreads the blame, and takes advantage of cooperative vibe that really generates the good stuff. Don't try to be Superman and do it all yourself.

3) **Lead By Example** - Show buyers why you have great products or a superior service, don't tell them. Don't talk about features, illustrate benefits. Demonstrate, don't describe - you'll be surprised how much more powerful your approach becomes.

2) **Good Enough In the Mail is Better than Perfect On the Drawing Board** - You can massage copy all day long, try different shades of blue until you're blue in the face, but it's not making you any money if it's not in the mail. That doesn't mean hurry through it, it just means don't worry it to death. Just by following the checklist presented here, accuracy and effectiveness will jump from 50% to 80%, and a little extra tinkering will get you moving toward 95%, at which point you reach the start of diminishing returns for the level of effort.

1) **Trust The Data, Listen to Your Gut, Value Others' Ideas** - It all comes down to pushing more work out the door and having it be productive, effective and impactful. Don't let ego make you an impediment to your own success. Keep fueling the idea machine with every resource you have, and you'll succeed in spite of yourself!

Be An Agent For Change

At its root, marketing is about change. Changing perceptions, changing appearance, changing buying behavior. But if marketers are to conquer the C-suite and earn a real seat at the management table, they have to be an agent for change in the business. Simply executing within the frame isn't good enough any longer.

It's up to us as marketers to lead the charge into the future, to examine and adjust business models, to question the status quo and come up with workable solutions, without reservations, obstacles, roadblocks, and excuses. Lots of platitudes surround this type of behavior, but the ones that I prefer are "Better to ask forgiveness than permission" and "If you're not moving forward, you're moving backward, there is no standing still." Food for thought . . .

Chief Marketing Officers have it within their power to revolutionize their businesses, they just have to give themselves permission to do it. Use the powerful imagination you were blessed with and put it in gear to create the next step in the logical growth path of your business, or better yet, leapfrog the next step and go ahead by two! The competition will never catch up!

Change effected is usually change managed. Making changes for change's sake is a short-lived phenomenon, one that shakes things up, but doesn't move the needle for long. To affect long-lasting change, the path must be plotted before it can be blazed. Note the word, "Plotted," not "Plodded." You don't have to take a year to plan the next two - change can be made quickly and still be lasting. Better to try five or six different things now than plan one thing perfectly.

Go forth bravely, boldly, and be a change agent - you'll be surprised what just the change in mindset will bring . . .!

Is Failure Life's Greatest Teacher?

Most of us don't like failure, in general, and largely feel that failure is bad. True entrepreneurs, and marketers can be included in this, often tout great failure in the past as the driving force behind their current success. They've looked at their past objectively, dispassionately, and impersonally, and taken strong lessons from the failures and used the knowledge to fuel success. It's a very healthy approach, but one that is often difficult to adopt in other circumstances. If you're not the boss, continual and ongoing failure in your work will not likely lead to a long career, unless you work at a Wall Street bank!

Failure is a terrific teacher. It shows you when you should have zigged when you zagged. And often, the ultimate failure of a business enterprise is not caused by any single event or decision - it's usually a cascade of seemingly small, inconsequential decisions and actions that take you down a path leading ultimately to collapse. If you could review any one of those decisions separately and out of context, you'd be hard pressed to find logical fault with it, taking into account its isolation and the information available at the time. But couple it with incomplete or inaccurate information that fills in or corrects later, and couple that with other seemingly innocuous decisions, and when you step back you can see a pattern developing. You can almost watch the slide in the wrong direction, but at the time you can't see it and are powerless to stop it.

Someone smarter than I once said, "It's not what knocks you down, it's how you handle getting back up that shows your true character." I firmly believe that to be true, being an optimist, and believe that this kind of thinking is what powers the entrepreneurial spirit that makes this great country what it is. No matter what obstacles people put in your way, no matter how many times they knock you down, if you just get up, brush off, restore your dignity, regroup and come out swinging with a new action plan, you'll eventually be alright and prosper. To do that repeatedly and not be insane, you have to examine the failures and learn from them to avoid repeating the mistakes that led to the failure.

My firm closed down an ancillary business unit this year, as it produced insufficient revenue to be self-supporting after two years of investments in time and money. The research told us we were right to launch it, the market should have been there, our advisers and others told us it was a great idea, but in the end, not so much. Now it's time to do the autopsy, find out what went wrong, and file it away so we don't repeat it in the future. Without this final, often painful, step, the failure has little positive value. Simply chalking it up to experience and loss without the analysis will only yield negatives. Eventually enough negatives can weigh your efforts irretrievably downward to the point of being unable to recover.

What's the recovery plan? Once the analysis is done, the lessons learned, the mistakes and missteps identified, we move forward in a positive fashion, richer in the knowledge that we can apply that learning not only to our own endeavors, but apply it on behalf of our clients as well. That's progress.

In short, don't hide from failures or hide the results when they are less than optimal. Own them, learn from them, and use them to your advantage. Those who say they only succeed are lying or selling something.

Tell the Corporate Story - Not "Just the Facts, Ma'am"

My associates and I have been reviewing lots of corporate materials over the last several weeks. Public corporations hold shareholder meetings, and issue proxy voting statements for the shareholders to provide feedback to the Board, elect new board members and settle other issues like compensation, accounting firm choice, and other matters. They are also required to bring shareholders up to date on the financial health of the company. Many of them choose this opportunity to further inform shareholders of their efforts and fill them in on future endeavors planned by the company, by mailing out annual reports with lots of artfully crafted text and full-page glossy images - all that's required by the Securities and Exchange Commission (SEC) is a set of edited, audited financials and some bare-bones intent reporting.

If you read this creatively crafted text carefully, you'll have a hard time discerning where the company fits in the competitive scheme in their industry (they're all industry leaders) and how their products are perceived, sometimes even what they do or are used for! Some are so nebulous, so vague, so "artful" and flowery, they become nearly useless.

Holy missed opportunity, Batman! What a tremendous chance to reach out and tell your corporate story in a way that really provides not only usable information that might prove relevant to increasing future investment, but to do double duty in a number of other forums where a corporate story might be useful. Love the images, too, but do they reflect the daily reality at that firm? Not likely. Do they tell the story? Better than the text, but is it the right story? Maybe not.

I think they can do better. Printed annual reports may be going the way of the dinosaur, with online websites allowing technology to improve communication's timeliness, and relevance. The use of multiple images, video, and the tantalizing prospect of nearly endless real estate in which to put more flowery copy, not to mention the reduced cost of reproduction and distribution, make online Annual Reports very tempting. I'm not sure of the SEC's feelings on this, but investors now have online proxy voting, so the annual reporting requirements can't be far behind.

For now, let's hope corporate marketing departments take transparency to heart, and while they don't have to back track all the way to the days of Dragnet scripts, a little direct, honest language may go a long way toward convincing shareholders to maintain and even increase their investment. It might also allow employees and other constituencies to become company evangelists - surely the current copy can't be repeated verbally by company representatives - at least, not with a straight face . . .

Key Marketing Element - Define "Value"

Whether we're creating a marketing plan, implementing a creative campaign or setting up for a key sales call, there is always a big question lurking in the background of all of our efforts - "What is the value of our product/service to the customer?"

Most marketers can create a list of features that show off their product, might even do enough to differentiate it from competitors, but features don't really drive response or sales. A list of benefits, what good things your product or service will result in for the customer is better, and will drive response and sales. But showing value, real intrinsic and perceived value, is where the true art of observation, listening, distillation and research converge to drive real results. This is where experience will pay off.

Take for example a simple cleaning service: the features they might offer include trained personnel, bonded service agents, natural or organic or hypoallergenic cleaning products, long-term contacts and one-time specials for realtors and landlords. But those features will make the reader work to derive the benefits from them, if you're lucky. More likely they will go on to the next competitor.

Benefits derived from these might include peace of mind for landlords and homeowners, high quality cleaning jobs above and beyond the normal, fixed and reasonable pricing, flexible scheduling for repeat customers etc. Good benefits, if you know you have a need and understand how such services work and the challenges that they can bring. Again, that's a lot of work for the reader to figure out whether this service is for him/her.

But what is the real value - a good impression on viewers or potential renters or buyers of the house or its residents, reduced risk of disease and infestation because the house is clean, reduced risk of allergic reaction due to reduced dust and allergens, and the bottom line - you don't have to put in the work to clean the house! People hire a cleaning service because they don't have time or expertise or inclination to clean it themselves. Luxury, convenience, time saving, thoroughness and a quality result are the key value triggers for marketing those types of services, so make sure you highlight them in your outreach efforts.

Those values can be derived from some quick customer and ex-customer research, maybe a card after the service is SOLD, not after services are rendered, that's a service-level evaluation, not a buying reason. Maybe a quick online survey or e-mail survey to your current and past customer list would reach the audience effectively. But you have to ask the right questions to extract this actionable information, and some analysis is needed to apply the newly derived data to your creative and strategic executions - that's where the experience comes in - a highly experienced marketer can do that distillation of data and analysis and derive a strategy based on that knowledge and execute it for real results.

Do your homework, do the analysis, and show the VALUE in your offering, not just features and benefits - value finds a home in buyers minds every time.

Leadership Behaviors Gain You a Seat at the Table

I've long been an advocate of soliciting the help of marketing experts when developing, launching, and branding new products, services or businesses. I've seen in our practice that the earlier you get the marketing folks involved in the process, the more likely you are to be successful. This is backed by study after study, both anecdotal and empirical, over the last 20 years. How many articles and references have you seen, including obituaries, that say something like ". . . successful business man was a marketing and promotions genius and applied his skills to creating and growing the company . . ."?

Clearly, the knowledge of the practice and theory of marketing is a valuable, nee critical skill to have in your bag of management tricks. And indeed, it seems the more input from the marketing folks you get, the faster and bigger the success is! Ramp up times are shorter, development and product lifecycles reduce, launches are more dramatic, and alternate applications and uses surface faster and are more often taken advantage of, when the marketers get heavily involved in the upper echelon decision making.

So why has it taken so long, and required so much effort for marketers to seek and achieve a true place at the C-level of management structures in the U.S.? The newly-invented Chief Marketing Officer title was a hard fought battle, typically one that is won on an individual basis, and in only a small percentage of companies, often larger and older firms, where upper management is often tinged with risk spreading behaviors rather than overt leadership. Often this battle is won by only the most vocal, dynamic, personable, innovative, and connected of marketers. One might say these are inherent traits in every good marketer, but you'd be surprised at some we've worked with who are impossibly poor at blowing their own horn while excelling at promoting the business they serve.

I'm convinced, after working directly with over 100 marketers in approximately the last thirty years, that those who market themselves as well as they do their firms are those destined to go the farthest. In some cases, it's a matter of the squeaky wheel getting the grease, but that only really works on an internal basis on the way up the ladder in a contained environment. But in this case, they have to not only talk the talk, they have to walk the walk, too. You have to back up the swagger with bottom-line success time after time to truly gain legend status. Just plain visibility alone won't do it.

Business executives rise to prominence in their own small world through long-term, solid achievement, aided by public recognition of those achievements and a desire to be associated with those achievements. Which makes it even more amazing that marketers have had such a hard time gaining celebrity status in the business world, as marketers have an endless series of "wins" to point to on a given day.

Some of the difficulty is that marketers tend to be collaborative, work in teams, even if the team leader works in a supervisory capacity - there's just too much for one person to really do without spreading the load, and thus the credit. CEO's get credit for the good decisions, and spread the blame for the bad ones among their top management team. Marketers tend to take it on the chin for the failures, while others take credit for the successes. That shadow tends to keep them in the background, slaving away as good corporate brand stewards, until there's a regime change.

The challenge before us as marketers is to show loudly and often the value we contribute to corporate success. We needn't be shy about putting our names and faces behind the successes we create, because in reality, there is no success in business without something being bought or sold, and we're the closest to the end of the sales chain and have the best understanding of what customers want and need. That makes our expertise not only critical but invaluable. Don't be afraid to step up and take credit for the successes, spread the credit as far as you need to, to your team and beyond, but accept the success for what it's worth without demurring or deferring. On the other side of the coin, never shirk responsibility for the inevitable misses, take them head on, learn from them and apply that education to the next situation. You'll be applauded and respected for the integrity, so you win anyway.

Stay the course, be visible, be effective, have an impact, and don't be afraid of public exposure - you've earned every last bit of it. Be the corporate leaders I know you are, but do it in a visible way. Everyone's a winner in the end when you do.

Innovation: Bravery + Curiosity + Support = Advancement

As Granite Partners' associates effect change at various client organizations, mostly through redirecting the current marketing efforts, we often encounter some underlying resistance from some of the down-line managers. Most of this has very little to do with our efforts specifically, and has much to do with aversion or resistance to change in general. We are change agents by nature, indeed that's the reason we are engaged is to effect change. If change wasn't needed, we wouldn't be there . . .

The question often arises, "How do we mitigate this resistance and achieve full consensus throughout the company to drive the program forward successfully?"

The answer often lies in two areas:

1) I realize that you can't please all the people all the time (to paraphrase John Lydgate), and there will always be dissenters and those who don't completely buy in to the new programs or processes. The way we've found success in handling those is to isolate, educate, reformulate, and redirect those individuals. This keeps them from spreading negative messaging throughout the firm, poisoning the well.

2) I understand that much of the atmosphere of innovation we are trying to create comes from the roots of corporate culture, and so that's where you start to effect the necessary changes.

That all sounds good on paper, but what does it really mean to client companies?

Like many such changes in corporate behavior, it all starts at the top. I work closely with CEOs so that they understand the impact of their downstream messages, and help them position the new elements in the proper light, so they can lead by example, both in action and words. Once the messaging of innovation is firmly established, it should be supported by new programs run by Human Resources, so that innovation carries an incentive and is rewarded. This clearly establishes the goals and guidelines for those individuals responsible for activating those new elements.

Once that infrastructure is in place, mid- and lower-level managers can be directed both by specific goal and by example, to help create the atmosphere that supports innovation, building competitive teams, setting an agenda that drives innovation and rewards initiative, and stresses accountability.

This trickledown effect needs to be championed all the way through the rank and file and out to customers, suppliers, vendors and support groups, so that it rings true no matter what angle the company is viewed from.

Go forth, affect change, champion the positive effects, and guide the culture and the results will follow!

Tips and Truths For Marketers

For those of you who are marketers, or if you're a business owner or solo prac-titioner who acts in a marketing capacity (and who doesn't), here's a few things I've picked up over the years - they don't have anything to do with social media, channel support, SEO or anything to do with a particular media.

10) If you've worked hard to evoke an emotional response to your product in an ad or direct mail piece, for goodness sake give people a way to actually buy it! Make the response mechanism obvious, it avoids delay in responding.

9) Put your address and phone number on your website, in an obvious place - not everybody trusts everything they see on the internet, and sometimes you just want to send somebody something or talk to an actual person. Why make me work at it?

8) ASK for the order. Don't assume that the audience will understand what you want them to do, no matter how obvious you think it is.

7) Take the offer seriously in your ads and direct marketing communica-tions - the audience will, and they will hold your feet to the fire for every possible interpretation you can imagine. The more transparent and clear you make the offer, the less confusion you'll receive from the audience, and confused audiences tend not to buy things.

6) Treat your customer and prospect lists like the gold that they are - you'll never find a more receptive set of eyes and ears for your message than someone who is already predisposed to hear it. Respect the power it represents, and the people behind it.

5) You can never know too much about the people you're trying to reach - but you can interpret data incorrectly. Take Ronald Reagan's advice, Trust But Verify, and vet your data with real people and anecdotes - you'll be glad you did.

4) Make your copy simple enough that your grade-school children can under-stand it. People's attention spans are increasingly short, and they don't have time to analyze your obtuse copy to extract your message.

3) Sales letters should be long enough to compellingly tell the story, and not a word longer.

2) Lists, design, artifice and devices don't sell products and services, feelings do. Evoke an emotional response in your audience and you'll move the needle.

1) A target audience never bought anything - PEOPLE buy goods and services - whether it's online, through the mail, over the phone or from a billboard. Reach out in an accessible, human way, meet a need or solve a problem, and the sales will follow.

Seems like basic common sense, but ignore such simplicity at your own peril. You'd be amazed how many top-flight professionals can't apply these basic tenets to their everyday work and score a good number.

Honesty . . . is Such a Lonely Word

With apologies to Billy Joel, honesty is becoming more of a requirement for corporate behavior than ever before. Transparency, honesty's trendier cousin, gets most of the glory in business circles, but basic honesty can go a long way toward truly influencing consumer behavior.

Companies who are honest with their customers, setting realistic expectations of their products, service and respect for the customer's intelligence and privacy, find that customers are more loyal, last longer, spend more on average, and are better brand evangelists, than companies who are less so. Might seem simple on its surface, but delivering on the promise on a global basis in your company is extremely difficult, unless every single employee is trained to think and react the same way, using the same basis for decisions, and respecting themselves and their customers, internal and external, at the same level. Tough to control, tougher to execute long-term.

A few iconic brands have managed it - Disney, L.L. Bean, Johnson & Johnson, and a few others come to mind. Every single employee must "drink the brand cool-aid" and live by the credo the company stands for, day after day, day in and day out. From the pick-and-pack temporary employee to the CFO, each employee must believe so wholeheartedly in the company's mission, in the company's inherent "goodness" and be able to honestly portray it in their daily lives, that they project that same ethos to everyone they meet, it almost becomes part of their personality.

More importantly, their corporate marketing and sales messages must be honest as well. That includes taglines and slogans as well. In a study performed through collaboration between University of Miami, Hong Kong, University and Haas School of Business at the University of California at Berkeley, study participants were asked about their brand preferences and spending habits as related to brands and to slogans. Their purchasing history and behavior were studied, and the results were quite interesting. Apparently for brands, there is a "priming" effect. When consumers are told that they are engaged with a "luxury" brand, they actually spend 26% more than they intended. When exposed to a "savings" brand, like Wal-Mart or Dollar Store, they spend 37% less than they might have otherwise. Clearly the priming effect of luxury being worth more is right in line with that. Now, here's the interesting part: Slogans attached to those brands work in exactly the opposite way. The inverse relationship is not direct, but it's a corollary relationship based on how honest the consumer feels the slogan is, how hard it is attempting to influence him/her.

After being exposed to a slogan designed to elicit spending (Luxury, you deserve it) they spent 26% less than after being exposed to a more neutral slogan (Time is What You Make of It). When the slogan invited participants to save, (Dress for Less, for example), they actually spent 29% more! What's going on here?

Turns out, the more participants thought the slogan's intent was to influence their behavior, trying to actually sell them something, the more negative the effect it had on their perceptions and on their spending as a result. The less "salesy" or influential the slogan, or the more honest they thought the slogan was, the more they spent.

Certainly there's no need for marketers to abandon slogans, but they need to assess whether the one's they've crafted work at cross-purposes to the brand. Public perception of corporate honesty has reached such a primitive and base level that mistrust is almost inherent. To re-establish that trust, companies need to present themselves in the most honest way possible. Their past behavior has trained consumers to "look for the catch" in every offer, distrust offers that involve any sort of mathematical calculation or savings scheme, and to automatically bypass offers that involve small print or asterisks and sub-notes. Sad.

The bright spot in all this is that honest, transparent companies now stand a real chance of succeeding in spectacular fashion now that the pendulum has finally swung the other way. This is a tremendous opportunity for new companies to set precedent, set a new standard, and to respect their customers' intelligence and emotional instincts, and incorporate those characteristics of trust and honesty into their brand promise.

Go forth and be honest - hopefully it won't be lonely for very long.

Engaging Customers – Modern Thought on Reaching the Current Consumer

Recent economic indicators describe a consumer climate that is different than virtually any in recent history, and consumer product and service businesses are having a tough time closing sales and encouraging sales traffic, both brick-and-mortar and online. This enforced stinginess on the part of consumers is widespread but not universal. Some products fly off the shelves and some companies are wildly profitable, while the majority seem to be pushing a rock uphill.

Consumers are caught in a vicious cycle economically, have been since 2008. Profit is down on a per unit basis, write-downs and charge offs notwithstanding. Employment is down from knee-jerk reactive cost-cutting measures trying to stem the tide of red ink, the unemployed numbering in the many hundreds of thousands, and the underemployed doubling that. Equities in general have been stumbling along the bottom of the trough for the last two years, with a 3% growth number putting them back at break-even since before the crash. Spending is down, savings are flat, foreclosures are restarting their relentless march, debt is way too high, both consumer and governmental, and consumers are cautiously nervous.

For retailers, this is the perfect storm of nightmares. Consumers are too scared to make those bigger purchases due to income uncertainty. Retailers won't or can't hire due to low margin, and can't add jobs, reducing the unemployment numbers. Investors get lousy returns, and therefore can't invest in riskier companies, so they can't expand and add jobs. Consumers who have jobs are unsure they will keep them, but are doing the work of three and trying to keep their own head above water, cutting back on discretionary purchases. So, as a marketer, how do you break through the fear and engage consumers? In a word, "Trust."

If you scan the list of most profitable or growing consumer product corporations*[1], you'll notice that they don't have a common theme in terms of product offering, or price point or position in the marketplace, although they all tend to be number one through four in their category. The common thread among them won't likely jump out at you from the list itself, but if you dig a little deeper, the theme becomes clear. These growing, smart, stable companies have been conservative in their growth plans, aggressive in defense and development of their brand, and firm believers in keeping their brand promise, leading to outstanding customer loyalty. They make products that people want and need no matter what their economic circumstances, and maintain loyalty through consistent quality assurance, product development speed and flexibility. In short, they give their customers what they want, and have done so long enough and consistently enough to have garnered long-term customer loyalty, and more importantly, trust.

[1] List compiled by Seeking Alpha, copyright 2010

As marketers, we can't often affect many of the attributes listed above that these firms have in common, but the few that we can, need to be the very best expression of the brand promise to establish that trust. We can't affect QA directly, for instance, but we can certainly pitch the promotions to the correct consumer level and keep public perception on the right aspects of the product if QA is spotty or suspect. Product development is sometimes seen as Indian territory for the marketing department, but in these high-profit companies, our studies show that marketers are deeply involved in not only accumulating consumer data to feed product development, but provide assistance and expertise on consumer preferences, brand extension and alignment, and even assessing product features and elements, to be sure they meet consumer preference and demand. Perhaps this characteristic above all others may be the critical element in the continuing romance between these companies and their customers. In almost every case, companies that get the marketing staff involved early in the development process and have a defined process for creating, developing and launching new products are more nimble, responsive and profitable than those who simply launch and market products after the fact.

That's great for companies that create a range of new products regularly or update their flagship product routinely. But what about some of those firms who have been riding the same product year after year? How do they engage their customers and engender such loyalty to the brand?

Many established and older brands that have let research and development languish, either through lack of resources or short-sighted thinking, find that they need to create or establish a new angle, a new application, a new extension of the existing product to create interest from new customers and renew interest from existing customers. Clorox might be an example of this, especially 10-15 years ago. Household bleach is a staple, has few innovations or moving parts, and aside from updating the package, and not much of that, it is basically unchanged since the 50s. Recently, they have innovated within the category, created new applications for the product and formed partnerships with other products to bundle or reinforce their products. Adding their product to other cleaning products gets the brand into households that might not welcome them otherwise, and sets or reinforces the expectation that bleach is an enhancer of cleanliness. Making the product "portable" in the form of a stain removing stick was a recent innovation that was launched in response to consumers' increased mobility and need for instant gratification. Yet despite its age, Clorox continues to move off the shelves in predictable and growing fashion and avoid becoming a commodity, despite strong shots from competitors, generic versions manufactured overseas, and reduced profitability from price increases on raw materials and distribution challenges. A marketing team that can come up with a new angle for a 50+ year old product is a strong, flexible one indeed. What has kept them going is strong customer loyalty, and trust in the quality and integrity of the product to perform as advertised day in and day out over many years.

But engaging customers doesn't always mean product innovation, or even marketing innovation. Sometimes it has more to do with taking the appropriate approach based on customer's expectations.

One of the companies on this list, Harley Davidson, is a champion at delivering its message in the most appropriate medium for its audience's digestion. But that hasn't kept them from being innovative to engage the customer. Over a century old, Harley's target customer is also getting older, and that demographic is populated by notoriously slow adopters of new technology. Harley does much of its marketing through the dealer channel and through event and sponsorship presence. They host rallies, rides, and other gatherings of product users through an extensive network of dealers and repair facilities coast-to-coast, and know their customer well. They have a huge array of licensed products and aggressively protect their brand in each of these arrangements, selecting only the highest quality materials, workmanship and designs to put their name on. This is one of the most traditional marketing models out there, and it still works very well. You would not expect them to have a huge online presence or use internet resources extensively to reach a 50+ age audience. Yet they have taken advantage of the social media phenomenon to help spread their message via word of mouth among their vast network of customers, creating Twitter accounts, a strong presence on Facebook with nearly 2 million friends. Other efforts include each dealer's own FB page and own website, all of which have access to the manufacturer's site, news, product info, dealer locator and more, plus license holder sites. All of this is used to promote new products, showcase product innovation, and get customer feedback, monitoring the electronic conversation and reacting quickly to customer input, engendering even greater loyalty and trust. It's the message, not the medium that counts.

Engaging customers also has to do with relevance. Being relevant to your customers may seem like everyone's goal, and indeed it might be, but these profitable companies seem to have it innately present in their corporate DNA. These companies constantly seek ways to enrich their customers' lives, and find new ways to be part of them. Coach, Inc., might be a good example of this. The luxury brand has innovated a number of approaches to meeting the needs of its niche market for upscale handbags and accessories, leveraging their brand strength over a series of related products. If you purchase a Coach bag, with its famous lifetime warrantee, and it's likely you'll be informed about other Coach accessories, and often buy them, with the assurance that each product, either direct manufacture or licensed, will be made with the same level of care and quality, and at the same price point in the market. If you are a Coach-level consumer, you make it your business to show it, by buying the branded products that prove it. This elite, exclusive approach works very well for them, as it ramps up the relevance in their customer's lives.

As marketers, we have a huge volume of information and research data available to us regarding consumer trends, preferences, and behavior. It is up to us to responsibly use this data on OUR customers, to craft innovative, trustworthy, relevant outreach messaging to engage our customers to create brand trust, and drive sales and profits to where they need to be. Most of that trust and relevancy comes from the correct and appropriate use of that data to craft messaging that resonates with the target consumer. Transparency, honesty, relevance and trustworthiness are key to achieving these goals, and you can see the results of such activity reflected in the marketplace and the bottom line.

Just Like Rodney, Marketers Get No Respect . . .

I've been reading and absorbing a lot of chatter about the level of respect marketing professionals get (or don't get) in companies across the nation. There is some debate as to how to justify and validate the need for such positions as Marketing Director and Marketing Manager - debates that tend to ignore the elephant in the room. The bottom line in most of these discussions is that if nothing is bought or sold, then there really is no "business," and that without the skill of folks internally in a marketing capacity, regardless of title, no one would be aware that the potential for commerce with your business exists, and therefore no transactions could occur. So, based on that logic, without marketing, there is no business. Yet, there is an ongoing debate as to why such people are needed, and what their value to the organization might be.

Why is this?

Is it because the rank and file are jealous that the marketing people seem to have all the fun - planning and attending big events, creating collateral, going on photo shoots, speaking with media editors and television stations, creating commercials, and the like?

Is it because other employees think they could do the marketers job, it doesn't look too hard and they have fun, so why can't I contribute to that?

Is it because with so many marketers out there, there must be a reason everybody picks that, it must be easy?

Is it because they have a larger budget to work with, and sometimes a larger staff over which to divide the work?

I've heard all of these postulated in one form or another, and many others as well. I've sat in meetings where senior executives questioned the efficacy of the entire marketing department's efforts in the face of 10-20% business growth directly tied to specific campaigns! When the economy slows, such complaints often rise in volume and stridency. Apparently a rising tide floats all boats, but when the waters recede, the marketers that made the boat and kept it afloat are no longer effective . . .

As marketers, it is our job to facilitate contact and commerce from without the company by working from within the company. There needs to be a belief that an investment in marketing activity drives commerce far in excess of its cost, and that beyond that, criticism of the mechanisms employed and the means brought to bear are so much sturm and drang from naysayers. If a culture of marketing is formed and supported at the top of the organization, and communication of those efforts within the organization is fast, accurate and appropriate, that culture will flourish and all members of the company will prosper.

So, how do we spread the word of such simplicity, and earn the respect we deserve as facilitators of transactional commerce?

1) Do the job well, and get results that can be measured and proven.

2) Stop worrying about who gets credit, or blame, and focus on results.

3) Closely tie effort to results, and promote those results in reasonable, detached fashion - leave the ego out, and just state the facts without the superlatives.

4) Drive the volume of effort upward - not all ideas are good ones, and not all executions are perfect. But the more you attempt, the more likely one will be a success.

5) Innovate new ways of thinking and doing that drive success. Open your mind to input from unusual quarters, and give it its due diligence. You never know where the next great idea will come from.

6) Show that the work you perform every day has value to the entire company, that everybody wins when marketing is effective.

When sales activity slows down and the economy contracts, many companies go into "emergency" mode, cutting costs, laying off workers, creating an environment of fear and uncertainty, and delaying or outright removing opportunities for innovation - exactly the wrong reaction in a crisis. Many companies have been operating this way since mid-2008, and after three years the fear has turned to something else, killing creativity, halting innovation, and limiting possibilities for success.

This presents an excellent opportunity for the marketing department to shine! Teach the others how to do more with less - we do it every day! Show others how to think and work your way out of a problem - we do it hourly! Tell others how to prime your thinking to view situations rationally with an eye toward exploitable opportunity - we do that constantly!

Give away the benefits of your talents as a marketer, and the respect you deserve will return to you ten-fold - that's a heck of an ROI in anyone's book.

"Relevance" The Only Buzz-word Still Relevant

Recently we were conducting some research for an association client, consisting of some preliminary phone group conversations with some of the association's volunteer leadership. The group had been furnished with some thought-provoking questions prior to the call, to sort of prime the pump so to speak, and they were very forthcoming and vocal on the call. Their answers and level of discussion revealed their passion not only for their industry and chosen profession, but for their association and their desire to see it grow and serve the needs of the industry.

As the call progressed, as in most such conference calls, several of the eight or so voices started to monopolize the conversation, but as they were providing some solid insights, I let the discussion roll on in this fashion for a few moments. All of a sudden, one of the participants, who we hadn't heard from for more than a couple of mono-syllabic agreements since the beginning of the call piped up with a long, eloquent, involved response to a piece of the discussion - the questions had gotten around to something RELEVANT to her, and she jumped in immediately to contribute.

As I thought back on the call later in going over my notes, I noticed something in the transcripts. These leading members of this group had used the word "relevant" in their discussion of their wants and needs regarding the association no less than 20 times in a 90 minute call! Clearly, they were calling for the association to pay attention to them and to offer something they found valuable, that they could use to improve their work, status or professionalism. In reviewing some earlier work with other organizations, it became clear that many of them have a sector of their constituency that gets short shrift in the overall scheme of things. In my experience, the cry for relevancy becomes louder the more homogeneous your group becomes, and the minority becomes smaller as a part of the whole.

For organizations serving a diverse population, the need to take into account multiple points of view, diverse needs, forces them to think more broadly, to offer benefits that fit a wide range of sub-sector's needs. When the group becomes more homogeneous and a small group stands off to the side, it becomes less and less cost-efficient to serve them with their own set of benefits and offers, to serve them in a way they are used to being served. This type of behavior is often a precursor to an association splitting into smaller, splinter groups, each with diverging needs and desires and expectations.

In short, the benefits offered the majority have failed to continue to be relevant to the minority group. Chances are, the main group's marketing efforts reflect this, and if not corrected they will start to see participation, purchase response, renewal rates, and all the other touch points they measure decline for this one small group. This lack of relevance can drive the entire organization into a negative spiral if not caught early and rectified.

So how do you fix the lack of relevance? In a word, research. Most organizations will tell you that "they know their members very well." It has been our experience that the more they say they know their members, the more they live by that assumption, and the *less* they really know the membership's needs, wants and preferences. This particular blindness seems to afflict trade groups more so than membership societies, but it applies to both.

If you want to know what your members really think of you, and your products and services, ASK THEM! You'd be surprised how readily they will offer their opinions, how honest they will be under the right circumstances, and often how simple their needs are to meet. Once their inputs are incorporated into the organizations behavior, the association will start to experience much higher total lifetime values across the overall membership, much better renewal rates, much less cost to keep members, much less spent on recruitment marketing, and that effect trickles down through almost all aspects of your organization, creating much better fiscal health and well-being throughout.

Organizations that regularly and routinely poll their memberships, that ask intelligent, probing questions, in order to spot shifts in perceptions, identify underserved areas, failing programs, and budding successes, will predictably do much better than those who feel that surveys and other research are "invasive" or "irritating" to the members, and only survey them once every couple of years with the same routine and detached questions. Get to know your membership segments for real, reliably and recently, and use the knowledge to shape your education programs, to craft your conference offerings, to guide your tradeshow approaches and themes, to guide your publications' editorial calendars, to adjust your website, to shift your media selection for outreach, and you'll be amazed how much more "relevant" you are to the membership - even the smallest segment you have!

Building Your Team - Looking for Folks Who Aren't You

There comes a time in most working professionals' life when they are tasked with something significant and asked to create or build a team to tackle it. For some of us, this can resemble the team-picking exercise we all got through on the school yard for kickball - with predictable results: poor cohesiveness, bad management skills applied inexpertly, a lack of motivation and poor morale. In short, the project sometimes gets done, usually by the strongest or most domineering two or three, leaving the rest feeling disenfranchised or segregated, negated or worse, and a less than optimal project outcome as well. This is not a recipe for greatness.

Those who take a more strategic approach sometimes fare better, but not always. Those who look good on paper, and have incredible skill sets and diligence to spare, may not work well with others, may not mesh with the overall "gears" of the group, may not parse out their skills in a way that the team appreciates. The results are similar to the above, but with bigger egos.

A viewing of the recent movie "Moneyball" reveals that business is not the only discipline where emotionally selecting co-workers can have negative consequences, but that even things that look good on paper may not work well in real life. The movie also illuminates the fact that there is a hidden "something" that all winning teams have that all the statistical analysis, investigative scouting, referral burnishing or other team-selection method will not reveal. There's a certain "chemistry" among winning teams that is difficult to duplicate, harder to engineer or manufacture.

One way to set the stage for this "Chemistry" is to find individuals with complementary skills, and personalities, and just enough commonality to let each be comfortable. Six big-ego, Type A personalities banging around in there is likely to be a disaster, just as five or six introspective, analytical introverts. But two or three of each, with a couple of "neutrals" to referee and act as the voice of reason, and things start to look more productive. Sometimes pushing everyone outside their comfort zone has positive results, because the "adversity" acts like a bonding catalyst, sets up an "Us vs. Them" mentality that motivates, coalesces, and helps the normally divergent skills and personalities converge to solve the challenge at hand, just to prove they can.

Really good teams at their root have a level of respect for the challenge and for each of the members that keeps things moving forward and fosters trust. The more difficult the challenge, and the more exclusive the team, the better this works. Setting the stage for this starts with the team's nominal leader, showing an even-handed, rational and realistic approach to how they handle the others.

Team-building has to be looked at from many different angles and good ones are effective on several levels. A group of professionals who respect each other and each others's talents and skills, and who also spend off time as friends, is a rare combination but can be a very effective one. There's a certain element of vulnerability that helps cement things a bit more closely when you've seen the other team members let their hair down a bit and you do the same, put yourself out there a bit and show another side of yourself - let them in, and have them let each other in, and that's where the "magic" seems to start.

Chapter Takeaways:

- Marketing is part science, part art, all effort. Marketing is about change, driving it, managing it, accepting it, creating it, putting it to good use, harnessing it. Those with a personality suited to the level of detail, the granularity of data, the curiosity of mind, the openness of thought, the dissatisfaction with the status quo will do well in this role.

- Marketing is about people. Creating successful teams is about managing skills, personalities, egos, and goals and motivating those involved to all pull in the same direction and accomplish the goal. Marketing is a team sport.

- Marketing is about creating a *planned* investment in building the organization and putting the firm or product in the very best light with respect to a prospective customer. A target market never bought *anything*, people buy things or join organizations.

- Marketing struggles with some misconceptions, including that it's easy, everyone can do it, its all about advertising, they have the biggest budget and have the most fun, and other myths abound. Additionally, those myths have gotten carried into the C-suite and have caused some credibility problems regarding marketing professionals among senior management. What should be a dynamic, highly functional and respected relationship is a strained, tainted, misunderstood power struggle. The best way to fix it is for marketing executives to continue to demonstrate their value and their contribution to the success of the organization, in measurable, meaningful, universally understood terms.

2) Research/Planning

Planning Tools You SHOULDN'T Use

Hopefully, if you're a corporate marketer, brand manager, marketing director or manager, you and your organization have a marketing plan that is reviewed every four months and updated, adjusted, reworked to maximize return on investment and protection and polish of the brand.

If you don't, you'd better get one.

Most folks work toward having that plan include several different ways to measure their progress or success, often on a monthly or quarterly basis. Good for them. Not everything is directly measurable, but there are some indirect measurements you can use to gauge your effectiveness. Use them. Always.

For those of you forming a plan, here are a few common things that marketers face when crafting a plan internally. Picture the planning meeting, and get a good assessment of the personnel included in that meeting. These are things you shouldn't succumb to from those in that meeting:

5) **"We did it last year and it worked."** Marketers are supposed to be innovative, progressive, forward-thinking. Before you even get to the "and it worked" part, you should have a response ready that shoots this down. If you're not moving forward you're going backwards. It's a new year, use it.

4) "Our competitors did it last year, and it worked." See above, plus how do you *know* if it worked? Unless you have espionage reports from inside the competing firm, you're guessing. Plus, if you've stooped to the level of stealing from your competitor, why bother planning at all, just steal theirs.

3) "We don't need new research, we know our customers." Contrary to popular belief, your "gut" is not a primary research method, and won't yield adequate or accurate data on your customers unless you have only one - you. Field intelligence is invaluable in helping to shape perceptions generated by research data, but if you use it as the basis of your planning, you're missing a large part of your potential customer base. Why guess, when you can KNOW.

2) "Customer Service only deals with whiners, we don't need to include their data in the plan." Customer service representatives and receptionists who answer the phone are a major source of information on your brand perception and characteristics. They are also key sources of information on the clarity, transparency and effectiveness of your sales pro-motion efforts. When the complaint call volume rises, it does so for a reason. Find out why, and fix it. Then take the list of those affected, and send them something nice, and ask them to tell their friends how nice you've been. Converting complainers to evangelists is a very effective way of expanding your reach and polishing your brand. Listen to the CSR traf-fic and respond quickly, and include that you will respond to each inquiry within a fixed period of time in your plan.

1) "We don't have results yet, but it looks like it's working." Some initia-tives take longer than others to bear fruit. Unless you're a start-up, you have at least some transactional data to work from, and can project results from that to gauge effectiveness of your previous efforts. If you really can't get a measur-able assessment on the impact of a campaign, don't build your new initiatives based on that one - you could end up throwing good money after bad. Your plan needs to be broad spectrum enough and flexible enough to work around such issues without affecting the whole program.

Now that you've killed off all the bad ideas in the meeting, you can entertain the new, innovative and intriguing ones that you've forced everyone to come up with by taking away their crutches.

Innovation - Courage or Survival Technique?

Modern corporations that want to grow and prosper must innovate to survive and differentiate themselves from the competition. Simple to say; not so simple to do.

Does your firm innovate? Are you a leader, first or second in market share in your vertical or industry? If so, you are likely an innovator in your arena. If not, you are likely a follower, and destined as such to toil away to maintain the status quo, fighting to find and keep customers, build sales, create and use buzz and maintain your brand.

Innovation comes in a variety of forms, some in internal structure, some in product, some in technique or offering. And it doesn't have to be something complicated. Sometimes the simplest thing is innovative. Just because it hasn't been done that way, doesn't mean it can't be, it's just that it seems so obvious, you think someone else must have thought of it before. Not always true!

Like most things, especially marketing, it all starts with research. Figure out what others are doing, and improve upon it. Find out what the audience wants, and give it to them. Find out what causes your customer's pain, and alleviate it.

Sometimes the research can be done within your own company. Talk to customer service, talk to reception, watch how customers react to things, listen to their grievances, hear their stories, see how they behave with respect to your product, or organization. They can tell you things about your company you might not know . . .

Innovation can create challenges. That's the point. You need an internal champion to shepherd the change created by the innovative approach throughout the company, to nurture it, to answer questions, to guide its development, to protect it from the nay-sayers. Innovation can start at the top with a visionary leader, but it needs buy-in from the top, and must have universal buy-in up and down the chain to succeed quickly and completely. Once that universal acceptance and understanding is firmly rooted, you'll notice that champions appear, and the organization as a whole starts to embrace and live the story of the new offering - transparency becomes paramount.

Once you've gone through this learning curve so you know the steps to innovation, you can apply them over and over again, creating an environment of innovation, keeping your company ahead of the competition, permanently!

Innovate, differentiate, and dominate! Sounds like a plan to me . . .

You Gotta Have A Plan!

After 30 years of helping commercial companies and non-profit organizations enhance their effectiveness through high-impact marketing efforts, I've seen some patterns develop. It appears that there is a correlation between how effective these companies' marketing efforts are, and wait for it, the specificity and thoroughness of their marketing plan. It's not budget, it's not necessarily vision, it's not brilliance in creative execution - it's how well they draw up a plan and stick to it.

Imagine a fighter pilot, maneuvering a $150 million aircraft (a small one), randomly, changing course whenever clear skies present themselves, dropping ordnance on whatever targets strike his fancy. He *might* hit the assigned target, at the right time, in league with others also scheduled to attack that target. But the odds drop precipitously with each misguided maneuver and missed "opportunity" bomb dropped on his way there. That's how some companies run their marketing operation, wandering from media outlet to outreach platform to new endeavor, without ever consulting the plan, if one even exists. This kind of rudderless marketing is nearly always doomed to failure, and results from a lack of vision, lack of discipline, lack of planning.

The best way to avoid this is to actually go through the often painful but always beneficial exercise of creating a specific, measurable, organized, well-researched and grounded marketing plan, and disseminating it to EVERYONE, so that all stakeholders are in sync and can be involved in carrying it out in an informed way. Make a plan, stick to it, carry it out aggressively, and measure your results routinely, and you'll be pleasantly surprised how much more successful your efforts will be.

There are loads of publications, books, blogs, etc out there to help you with this task if you work for a young start-up with no experience at planning. Each one is different, each is unique, but each share several key elements, including measurable specific goals, time milestones, assigned responsibilities, and available resources. Fully complete plans include media choices for outreach advertising and PR activities, brand characteristics, audience profile, media schedules for placements, creative cues for progressive campaigns, drop dates for mail, e-mail, and designated resources and personnel for all tasks including social media activity.

Big job, but one that not only saves time and money over the year by reducing missteps and waste, and one that removes the guesswork and allows everyone to move forward confidently and aggressively toward achieving the goal. How simple is that? Apparently not very, based on a recent study* showing that nearly 40% of businesses with over 20 employees have no written marketing plan!

If you need help, get it. If you can't find it within, hire it! If you can't stick to it, post it and have someone else hold you accountable. Ultimately, it's plan now, or pay later - your choice.

*Study commissioned by Marketing Sherpa.com in 2011

Research Is a Cost-Effective PR Tool

All of Granite Partners' consulting engagements involve some sort of primary research, either as part of a 'Strengths, Weaknesses, Opportunities and Threats' (SWOT) analysis to assess market position, or customer interviews or surveys, or investigations into new applications for existing products. But there are other uses for empirical research - one of those is for PR media exposure.

If your company does field research, product development, manufacturing, or offers a service, you might be able to use your own internal corporate data, and publish your findings as they apply to the general public, and promote those findings to increase awareness of your company.

Generally, for a business to receive media coverage, they need to craft and offer a story that is timely, urgent, relatable and relevant. Under the right circumstances, research findings can be all of that and more. If you've invented a new chemical formula for use in your products, there is likely extensive research on that new formula regarding its safety, its physical properties, its applications, its effects when reacting with other substances, and a host of other attributes. If you look at those results in a slightly different way, you might find that there is news in that innovation. If you were to find that the new formulation enhanced lubrication between plastic parts, for example, or had other solvent properties when used against marker or crayons, or some specific stain, that product could be marketed to a whole new audience. Your research might be promoted as something like "**New Formula Removes Crayon Like Magic - new Kid-Safe Formula.**"

Take it further, if you are a service company, say a cleaning service, and you regularly poll or survey customers after they've received their service. Typically, there would be questions regarding the customer's satisfaction with the job, what they liked and didn't like, did the operators do a good job, did they arrive on time, etc. It would be very easy to add a couple of questions to that survey regarding the use of organic cleaning products, favorite fragrance used in the cleaning process, how the customer gauged the "level" of clean achieved, and others. In aggregate, that data could easily be used in an eye-catching headline "**Only 35% of Consumers Prefer Organic Housecleaning Products - Majority Feel Organics Offer Reduced Effectiveness**" and the subsequent release copy could go into detail about how customers don't show a preference for organic cleaners, citing that they don't clean as well, based on your own company's primary research. It's not a scholarly, peer-reviewed journal article, it's not a scientifically-vetted study, but it's honest, it has actual customer data included, and it shows a preference that might surprise readers - and what it really does is create a platform for you to gain some exposure for your company as a thought leader in the industry.

Granite Partners' consultants found in our experience with clients that primary research always pays for itself in terms of marketing insight, and some data has revealed trends, shifts in perception, and new applications that have yielded millions in sales and new growth for the companies that initially commissioned the research. Forward-thinking companies usually understand the value of the data we uncover, and the most innovative among them use that data for multiple purposes, including those described above. When weighed against all the additional uses for the facts that the data reveals, research is one of the most cost-effective marketing tools you have in your toolbox. Take a few minutes one afternoon and review your internal corporate research data on your products or services or customer's buying behavior, and see how many attention-grabbing headlines and stories you can wrench out of it - you might be surprised at the resources for media coverage you'll find hidden there!

Keep Your Audience Close . . .

As a marketer, I have a certain level of curiosity about my client's customers, and how to reach them effectively, how to reach their emotions, to shift their perceptions, to alter their behavior in a way that helps them make the decision to buy, to join, to attend, to engage in some way. That curiosity is at the heart of all of our engagements, and as a research-based marketing strategy purveyor, we get to indulge that curiosity on behalf of clients every day, and after some discussion realized that we were all grateful for that.

Knowing your audience thoroughly and as completely as you can is what makes for marketing success. It allows you to speak directly to them in your copy, it allows you to offer them products and services and opportunities that you KNOW they will appreciate and will feel entitled to obtain. Knowing what they like, when they are likely to like or need what you offer, knowing what stage of life they are currently inhabiting, and being able to predict how they will react to a given opportunity allows you to present thing you have to offer in a way that other retailers and marketers can't touch. Good research will allow you to do that, no matter what you're selling.

Many of our engagements involve outreach in the form of direct mail, which allows clients to reach a wide audience with customized offers or pricing or product choices created specifically for that individual or group of individuals, with remarkable success. Mail may seem antiquated in an era of high-speed social media, e-mail marketing, wireless mobile this and that, but really marketing is not about tools, it's about connecting with the potential buyer in a way that influences them. It's about influencing them to consider your products and services for purchase. Purchases make companies money, period. So really, all the online communities, all the digital social interaction, all the sharing of consumer information really doesn't make anyone any money until someone actually buys something.

What it can do is help you know your audience better. All the data served up voluntarily on a daily basis can help you frame a profile of your audience that's more true to life than what magazines they read or what type of car they drive, and certainly provide more recent information. The combination of social media data and transactional data from retailers can be an unbeatable combination for marketers hoping to know their audience better. The data is available, now you have to figure out how to actualize it, to monetize it, to turn data into dollars.

The more you know about that target segment and the individuals contained within it, the better you can offer them goods and services they will find appealing. If it's appealing, they will find a reason to buy it. The simple formula goes:

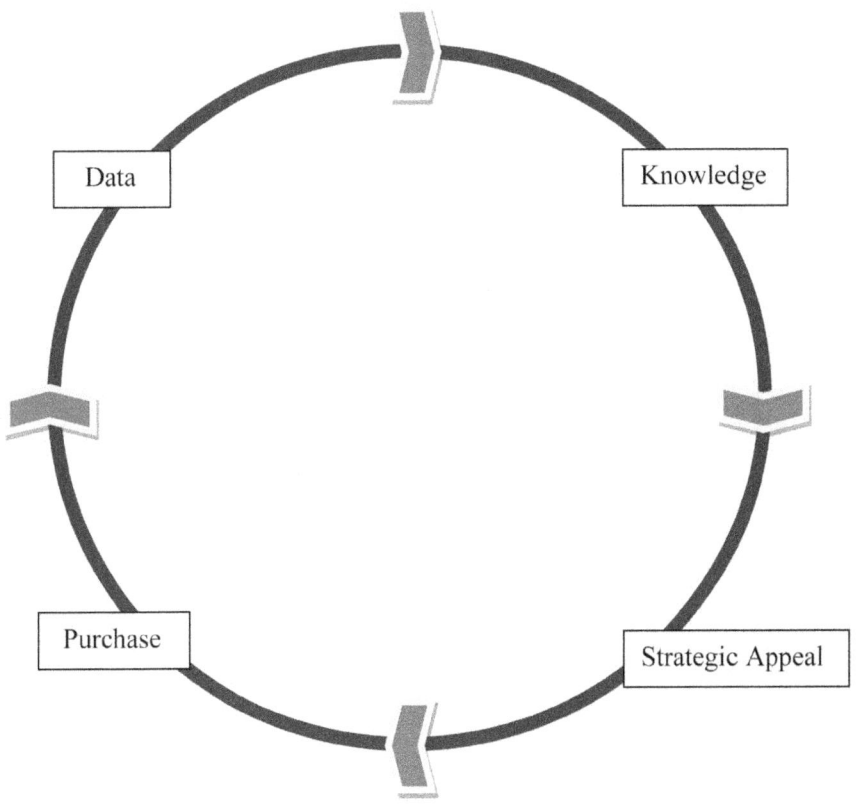

. . . in a big circle. It's a good formula to keep in mind, and it feeds into the whole idea of creating a community. What makes a community, in marketing parlance, is that you have a group of individuals who have a reason in common to repeatedly participate in a certain activity, be it buying, or discussing, or learning about or something involving what you have to offer. The "in common" part makes it efficient to reach them and binds them together. The "repeatedly" part is what connects you to the data acquisition formula, and what gives marketers the "in" to offer them things they find appealing over and over again.

The real moral of the story is that the better you know your audience, the better you can serve them and the better your marketing will be to them, which in turn adds to your ability to serve them. Go forth and gather data . . . you'll be glad you indulged your curiosity!

Chapter Takeaways:

1. Research is an invaluable business tool, and using it to inform marketing decision-making is critical for truly customer-centric organizations.

2. Strategic planning is critical for success, at it's core, research-based forecasting, goal-setting and activity planning all rolled into one. It is crucial to couple the plan to some research, and to couple that data to action instructions.

3. Good planning is required for marketing success, and once the 'research data, planning, execution, transaction, data' cycle is set up, it becomes self sustaining and self-actuating, rolling onward constantly fine-tuning the approach, messaging, targeting, and product development to fit customer

3) Sales

Key Cost-Saving Measure - Fire Your Customers

Smaller businesses have been affected disproportionately by the recent recession and rocky, slow, volatile recovery. One reason may be their restricted access to working capital via hometown banks, and another is that their cost-cutting measures might be incomplete. You might think you've cut costs to the bone, laid-off all the non-critical employees, and started reusing paperclips, but have you examined your customer list?

One of the toughest things for a small business to do is to fire their customers. Not all of them, obviously, but the "bad" ones. If you're in a service business, you almost invariably have bad customers - you know the ones I'm talking about - they pay late or not at all, they order endless changes, renegotiate contracts halfway through the engagement, ask for extras that don't get paid for, take up lots of unneeded customer service time, and their total spending during the year is wildly disproportionate to their attention needs. These are profit soakers, intent on killing margin, monopolizing executive, sales and customer service time, and are actually costing you money. FIRE THEM!

Unless you have empirical evidence of them referring magnificent amounts of new business your way, or evangelizing your services to everyone they meet, they aren't doing you any good, and you should refer them gently to another supplier. There's no reason to keep them around - if you like them personally, play golf with them, send them gifts at Christmas, but don't take their business, it's killing yours!

If you examine your customer list carefully, you'll almost certainly find a few that should be fired. Here's a quick way to locate them. Sort your list by annual spending, how much they actually paid you last year. Take the bottom 25% of that sorted list, and run it against the timecards of your sales people, Customer service reps and lead account people for the same period. My guess is that there are several of the lower 25% near the top of the resulting cross reference. Those are the time and profitability soakers and should be FIRED!

If your business follows the 80/20 rule, that 20% of your customers are providing 80% of the business, you could probably drop off the lower 1/3 of the list and be pretty safe. My suspicion is that if you do that, next year's financial statement will be much healthier, your sales and account people will have more time to prospect new business and open new accounts, attack new markets, and your bottom line will be much more robust.

Donald Trump didn't get so popular by being nice - he's made firing people an art. Don't shy away from this critical business responsibility and boost your bottom line!

Sometimes Business Growth Doesn't Mean More Customers

In my daily consulting practice, we see the inside of businesses all over the country, and can make some fairly educated observations about how they run. Small businesses especially are having a tough time running smoothly, in a couple of aspects, operationally and financially.

Smaller businesses, especially service businesses like landscapers, technology companies, contractors, painters and other building trades, are having trouble securing loans from local banks to use for working capital or expansion, new equipment, bigger crews, more workers. This type of business often has ebbs and flows in cash availability, either due to seasonality of their business or the size and nature of their work and their customers. Occasionally they need some extra capitol on a short term basis to make payroll and keep good people on the employee rolls until they are needed for the next big job. If they can't get that extra money, they are forced to cut other staff, benefits or worse, close down temporarily. This up and down cycle, when not mitigated by some cash flow injections, can eventually destroy a small business, even one that is well managed.

Operationally, this cash flow issue changes the dynamic among the core of employees, and causes the other problem this type of business faces: scarcity of qualified staff and an employee pool too shallow. If the threat of being laid off comes repeatedly to the rank and file, word spreads in the industrial community and you will have a hard time recruiting good employees. The stress caused by the impending downsize can negatively affect productivity, loyalty and other critical areas of performance.

That lack of cash flow can also have a negative effect on management decisions as well. If you're not sure you can fill that cash gap, but have receivables out there and the next big job is in the pipeline, management will still be reluctant to hire additional employees even when they're needed. This reduces risk-taking, limits growth and expansion, and slows movement among the employees. Mentoring behavior slows or stops, training dries up, and the whole works can come to a virtual standstill, largely out of fear of that "big job gap."

The third but highly overlooked issue for small businesses these days is making the transition from founder-lead, to goal-driven enterprise. Usually smaller businesses are started by a single individual, who has a skill or a talent. They are successful using those skills and the business grows. They hire some semi-skilled workers to help in specific areas, but the founder still acts as president, chief cook and bottle washer, wearing a huge number of hats on the managerial and administrative side, and still doing the principal work at the same time. If they get caught in this loop for very long, performance suffers, crucial but routine administrative work often gets missed or lies fallow for long periods, customer service suffers and eventually work quality will suffer.

The way to break the cycle is for the owner to know when it's time to find a trusted team to run the jobs and they move over to take a more strategic role. It's a different skill set, but one that can be learned. Finding that team is becoming increasingly difficult, and this is one of the biggest single issues facing small businesses and impeding their growth. Advice for job-seekers out there - look at your skills and experiences and frame them in such a way as to make you attractive to someone seeking a clone of themselves - make yourself appear trustworthy and indispensable, and you'll get hired in a second.

Growth from within, building a team, creating a chain of command, putting in place a management structure and policies that foster growth, innovation, initiative and empowerment are just as valuable as building up the customer list, and are a form of growth on their own.

Converting Prospects to Members (or Customers)

One of the biggest challenges non-profits and other small to mid-size businesses face is converting leads to sales, or for non-profits, a common challenge is to convert prospects to members. There are many different ways to approach this issue but they usually have a few things in common.

If you have a good list of well-qualified prospects, compiled recently, with a high-deliverability quotient, and fresh information, you're already halfway there. If not, but wish to start compiling one, there are several good ways to do that, including referrals from current members, industry indexes and directories, publication lists, and prospecting campaigns at tradeshows.

If you have e-mail addresses, this might be the least expensive place to start. If not, you're left with mail or phone campaigns to reach out to prospective members. If you have a really solid profile of your members, based on research, and can categorize them accurately into industry segments, title profiles and other segmentation to make your communications more specific. One factor to consider when making your selection is based on that profile, how do your current members like to be communicated with? Are they technologically astute, do they stay at their desks all day and have constant access to e-mail or social media? Do they only read e-mail at home? Do they get their mail at the office or did they give you a home address? The method deserves almost as much consideration as the message, in these highly overloaded, busy times. It's too easy to delete, discard or filter out messages delivered in inconvenient ways.

Once you've decided on the best medium, now you have to craft a message that resonates with this group or groups. Your research profile will be of great use here, as it tells you what they are likely to be concerned about, what issues hit home for them, what keeps them up at night. Once you've discovered that key issue, now you can formulate a message to deliver that shows how their membership will take care of that pesky problem, solve that challenge, meet that need and make joining a solid investment. Solve a problem, and you'll get them to join up just for that - show them the unique value of your organization in solving that problem, they'll stay members for years.

Now you just have to mate the message with the right medium at the right time and deliver it cleanly, accurately and in timely fashion. But before you hit that "send" button or pull the trigger on the mail drop, make sure your customer response, receipt, fulfillment and registration infrastructure is in place, and ready to accept the new influx of calls/e-mails/hits/members - there's nothing more frustrating than receiving inquiries or orders and not being able to activate them or monetize them - it's a woeful tale of opportunity lost. It's not overly optimistic to expect good response to your offer after taking the time to craft it so thoroughly and specifically. The better your homework and more thorough your preparation, the more likely you are to generate significant response and you have to have the structure in place to accept them.

Find your best list, do your homework, know your prospect, find out what they need, show how your organization can solve their problems and make life easier, get them the message in a form they're receptive to, and make sure you can accommodate all the requests quickly and efficiently. If you can pull those elements together, your chances of success soar, and so will your organization!

Networking Events Can Produce Results, But Common Interest Cements Relationships

We've all been there . . .

You go to an event, be it a conference, a seminar session or annual meeting, and you meet different business people, discover some common ground outside the theme of the event, and you keep in touch for a while after the event, but unless you work at it and nurture it, that relationship fades into the background, not serving either party. Occasionally, you run into someone that really has a lot in common with you, has some business reason to stay in touch and that relationship grows and flowers and produces solid business gains for both sides and lasts years. What made the difference?

I have a theory, and statistics gained in Granite Partners' work promoting events will back this assertion up to a certain degree: "The more closely aligned the business goals of the parties are, the less likely they are to form a longer-term relationship." On the surface that may seem counter-intuitive, but keep reading.

What drives business relationships is gain - profit, cash flow, commerce. Each side has to have a clearly defined role and those roles need to be complimentary, not unidirectional, for the relationship to be productive. Gains are made and money moved when something is sold or bought. Seven times out of ten, what drives that relationship is the desire to sell to the other guy! Two salesmen can get together and banter and share a beverage, but chances are that relationship will develop a competitive or adversarial nature. But if one is a salesman and the other is a mid-level executive in another role, something can be sold there, business moves, transactions done, and the relationship works for both. Two top executives can get together and share common issues, maybe even work on the same committee to solve an industry problem, and if there's no chance of them being in a competitive situation, and with nothing personal underlying it - tough conditions to fill - that relationship might come in handy from time to time, but it probably will not be terribly productive. No chance to sell to the other one! No chance to beat the other one, either.

Networking meetings in general have been overused and relationships forced upon business people for a long time, and they still serve a useful function, especially for those new to an area or industry. But without the quantity of time required to care for and nurture those relationships, and a good business reason to do so, in today's superficial and time-starved environment, most are short-lived and unproductive. The way to get the most out of networking meetings is to introduce yourself to a few key people, or better yet, have someone else introduce you to a few key individuals, and take the time to investigate them further, see if they are worth pursuing, and take the lead in keeping them fresh and alive. If you meet ten people and stay in touch with just one really solid business individual and keep that relationship growing, you can consider that meeting a success. At that build ratio, you'll need to attend a significant number of meetings to start a functioning network from scratch. But if you put in the time, make the investment in your own business future, you'll find it pays off in spades over the years.

The best technique that we've seen success with is to let such relationships develop naturally through outside interests other than business. That fellow soccer coach, that neighborhood association committee member, that dinner companion of a college friend, that last-minute fill-in in your golfing foursome, that guy who has season tickets right next to yours at the stadium or the theater - that's how relationships get started, and have no surface business purpose, but after getting deeper into them, you find common business ground if you're open to discovering it. It's old-school, but it works! It's less contrived, less forced, more comfortable for everyone, and you don't have to go out of your way, or wear a name tag for them to be productive!

Next time you're at a networking function where the specific reason for attending is to meet other people to do business, think back to other similar situations and count the number of people you regularly do business with, and ask yourself how many of them you met at such an event. The answer will likely be Zero! Now examine those same people you regularly do good business with, and ask how you met them initially. The answer is usually that you were introduced by someone you both knew from somewhere else.

Try this at your next social outing or sporting event: try and steer the conversation you're having so that it includes no clue about what your job is or what business or industry you're in. You'll be amazed how difficult it is, and how intriguing it makes you to others. But think of the information you've gathered. Now you know more about them as people, and can make a more informed decision about whether to pursue that relationship further, and find some common business ground. My guess is that the resulting business relationship will be stronger and last longer than the one derived from the forced, contrived situation at the hotel.

The Battle Between Sales and Marketing Rages On . . .

There are many areas of ongoing controversy in the world - Alien v. Predator, King Kong v. Godzilla, Greece v. Turkey, Israel v. (Pick one) and Sales v. Marketing.

I'm not going to come down on a side for most of the above, but the Sales v. Marketing one intrigues me, because the two combatants should be best friends. They share a common goal, they have separate methods and approaches, they both want more customers. They do compete for financial resources in some companies, so that may set off some minor turf scuffles, but I think each is misunderstood by the other, and it's a case of walking a mile in the other guy's shoes.

Add to this the fact that management executives in many companies confuse the role of each in their organization, in fact use the terms interchangeably. This kind of thinking simply adds to the controversy, and pits one against the other.

The functions are different, they have different ways of measuring success, have different individual goals on a small scale, and use resources differently. In some firms, the sales function is placed underneath a Vice President of Marketing, correctly or incorrectly depending upon the structure of the company, its size and the product or service being sold. My guess is that if that VP had to actually go out and sell to a lead list, they would not fare very well. That doesn't make them an inappropriate manager for that function, but it does weaken the case for non-peer review. On the other hand, if the leading salesman were asked to assess the company's current brand health, determine their most likely next move in entering a new niche vertical, or have to craft an outreach marketing strategy, they would likely come up with something that might have some value, but not the whole ball of wax.

The reason is that they are different skill sets, not interchangeable and with different focus points. The salesman focuses on customers one at a time, creates and environment where they can use their powers of verbal or written persuasion to tell people what they want to hear about the product in a way that motivates them to make a purchase, big or small, right then and there.

The marketer is in the mass communication business. They set up a virtual environment in the mind of a predetermined prospect type without ever having met them, make a case in a variety of ways for that product or service being the best choice among many, and motivate through written or spoken word (radio or television) to create an impression that drives huge numbers of prospects to understand that product or service in a certain way, and helps them decide to make a purchase at some point.

Success is determined for the sales person by dollars driven in, or clients gained, or products moved. Success for the marketer is about more products moved over time, a rise in brand awareness, the number of conference attendees at a tradeshow, and a host of other metrics determined by the goal of the exercise.

But these two can each do their job better in the presence of the other! They should be buddies! But they're often at odds within the organization. They each think the others' job is less important, likely because they've not done the others' work for any length of time. But by working together, they can each improve.

Sales, you need to understand that the marketer's mindset is more focused on hitting the most common denominator the most often, because it's easy for prospects to ignore their messages - delete them, throw them out, hang up, you name it, it's a one-way conversation. Marketing, you need to hold onto the understanding that if the prospect hangs up on or ignores pleas for a meeting, Sales takes it personally, because each one counts for a lot! They invest a lot of emotion and time into each approach, planning, investigating, researching, so they "know" the prospect much better - therefore when things to get accepted right away, it's a bigger loss.

A little understanding goes a long way. If Marketing took the challenges Sales faces to heart when creating one-sheets or promotions, they'd be simple, answer the most often asked questions, and be nearly weightless so the briefcase-carrying arm doesn't drag on the ground at the end of the day. If Sales realized how much time it takes to say things in just the right way, how hard it is to determine what the most often asked questions are, and how long it takes to "just redo it", they'd make their wishes known early and often, and get better tools to work with in return for their efforts.

We can't fix Greece v. Turkey, or even know whether it's Godzilla or King Kong that wins the battle for Tokyo, we do know that when Sales and Marketing work together things go much more smoothly and there more money all around.

Human Resources Are Your Finest Resources

Granite Partners' consultants get asked for advice and guidance by firms large and small every day, and when reviewing whether or not to work with a new client, we try to do our due diligence and determine for ourselves whether this going to be something beneficial for both client and consulting firm. One of the unspoken, immeasurable, but over-riding factors we consider is: "Do we like working with these people". The human factor is an "X" factor that is hard to quantify, but is crucial to a successful outcome.

How do you find, and keep those "Good" people in your organization, the ones that are loyal, hard-working, dedicated and passionate about their work? Top talent requires top treatment, but how do you craft an incentive program that keeps them challenged, interested and passionate? What kind of carrot do you dangle in front of those talented executives to keep them in your stable?

According to some of the region's foremost Human Resources experts, a one-size-fits-all approach to benefits, incentives, and retention is no longer viable, and I tend to agree. If you think about it, as marketers, we know that you can't expect great results by sending the same package to wildly different audiences. So why would you expect great results making the same offer to a broad range of employees? Internal segmentation is just part of the story. If you dig deeper, you'll find there are other elements that add to retention that you might not have thought of. Transparency is a tough issue that many private or family firms struggle with, but that can make a huge difference in your retention of top senior executive talent - they are savvy enough to want to know where the money is going and how decisions are being made that affect the future of the company. The lower- and mid-level employees should share this access to information, but for them, some more intensive and extensive education is coupled with the information, so that they can understand what they are seeing and how to interpret the data accurately and draw reasonable conclusions.

Most of the experts agreed that while retention is an issue, making good hiring decisions in the beginning is the single largest factor in keeping good talent on board. Some suggest pre-employment screening tests and inventories of various stripes, but most agreed as well that any single instrument should not be weighted too heavily, and certainly not weighted above the interviewers insights and impressions, background checks and due diligence. In general, their feeling was, skills can be taught, attitude cannot, and that those with the right mindset that will fit in culturally with the mission and goals of the organization will do better long-term than those with top skills but behavioral issues.

What does any of this have to do with marketing? It strikes me that there are parallels between how you select and retain employees, and how you attract and retain customers. Aside from the obvious connection that the marketing department personnel are crucial hires for your organization, and often some of the highest turnover. Good marketing talent is difficult to find, even at a point where double digit unemployment is quickly becoming the norm. If you find such individuals, you should strive to assess their needs and hold on to them using any means necessary, because they can make or break your company faster than any other department. Marketers can do more damage with a slipshod approach than any embezzler or bull-in-a-china-shop manager.

Spend as much time on hiring your marketers as they do segmenting their customer lists and researching the target market, and all will be well. Spend time to get to know them, make sure they're compatible with your mission. Don't worry if they seem a little "off" in a couple of social areas - these top talents are trained to think way outside the box, to innovate, to be renegades, not to be the round peg in a round hole. Don't hold that against them in the hiring process, for these are signs of their future success . . .

Engagement Means Understanding

Granite Partners has been working with several Business-to-Business clients recently on outreach programs to help them find and engage new customers, and one of the tactics we've had success with is the use of dimensional mail. The main reason is that while overall mail volume is down in the last two years, the amount of mail reaching top executives is up slightly, as gatekeepers have been removed through attrition or layoffs as company's pare staff, and we were finding that we needed to break through the clutter in the C-suite to get noticed and to actually engage these busy executives with our message.

While the list is still king, the package is gaining in importance. We're not talking about a simple A-B test between red and blue carrier envelopes, we mean a full blown package - a box of some type - that contains illustrative media, video, audio, print collateral or other physical, three dimensional object that requires time and thought to understand. It takes a few moments to open, to pick through the parts, to see the story unfold as you peel away layers and get to the meat, the point, the main message. Once you get there, it's got to make sense to the recipient, to be relevant, to be personal in a way that says "hey, these people know my business and are here to help me run it better!"

Personalization plays a large part in these packages. Good use of personalization has been shown to boost response significantly, and the combination of personalization and three-dimensional engagement means your target spends a good deal of time with your message, enough to thoughtfully consider your offer and put it in the "investigate further" pile. Now, it's time for the follow-up!

The dimensional package is a great way to bait the hook, it's intriguing, interesting and gets people thinking about your message. It may not be enough to close the sale by itself, few B-to-B direct marketing packages are, when there's a service or high-ticket item in the mix. But by pushing personalized, strategically-timed follow-up messages through different media, your product is now what we call "Self-vetted" - it appears to come from a variety of directions, and sources, so that it appears to be very safe, legitimate and reasonable. Since top executives are generally a conservative bunch, financially and emotionally, this plays on their natural caution and lowers their defenses, usually enough to make them receptive to a phone call, which is the knock-out punch of the campaign.

So far this scheme is working for clients, and we have several variations in the works, tweaking timing, packaging, levels of personalization and frequency. The key to effective execution of these campaigns is the homework you do on the list of recipients - each of these packages represents a significant investment by direct mail standards, and you want to keep your waste level low and your responsive recipients ratio as high as possible. Better to send out five and have two hit with real sales, than to send out 20 and have that same two hit.

A good list, an intriguing, personalized package, heavy follow-up and a persuasive phone call may seem like a lot to go through to reach a handful of individuals - but if they're the right individuals and the sale is worth thousands or tens of thousands or more, the discipline and forethought is certainly worth it.

Show Up, Suit Up, Follow-Up - Don't Forget That Last One!

Until now, I have focused on marketing strategy, tactics and practices, but I wanted to touch on a more sales and management-oriented topic that has been rearing its ugly head recently - Poor sales personnel practices.

If you're in sales as a profession, there are a few simple adages that pave the road to success.

1) Know your market, know your customer, solve their problems, don't create them
2) Under-Promise and Over-Deliver
3) It's more effective and less expensive to keep your existing customers than to find new ones
4) Always make that last call of the day, no matter how tired or late you are
5) Show Up, Suit Up, Follow-Up

If you can keep those things in mind as you go about your daily interaction with customers and prospects, you probably won't go too far wrong.

Where most less-experienced folks tend to drop the ball is on numbers two and five. Most new folks are so eager to make the sale, they will tell prospects virtually anything to close them, and then when it comes time for the order to arrive or be fulfilled, the customer is left disappointed or worse, feels cheated. At extreme levels this amounts to bait-and-switch, which is a prosecutable offense. You may get a few orders this way, but there won't be any referrals or recommendations, and the gravy train will grind to a halt fairly quickly, especially in the age of Internet postings, blogs and rating sites for every business imaginable. Word will get out even more quickly and nobody will touch you after that - bad idea.

Number five is sometimes a function of time management, sometimes of lack of training, sometimes lack of personal responsibility. The Show up and Suit Up portions, most have down, although I've spoken with many business leaders in the last few months who say they can't hire staff that can manage to do even that on a consistent basis. It's the follow-up that eludes most people, and the one's that discover this little secret are going to move to the top of the heap rather quicker than his or her competitors. Just because someone was not in a position to buy when you left them last, (some more hardcore folks would say you failed to effectively close them the first time) doesn't mean that they never will have a need for what you're offering. Your odds of them calling you when the time comes have much more to do with top of mind awareness and initial impressions than of product quality or benefits.

Effective follow-up must be gauged carefully and is different for each prospect. The tone, medium, frequency and content of your follow-up are critical to maintaining that tenuous connection and reinforcing that initial, hopefully good, impression. The more personal and more specific you can make that follow-up, regardless of the medium, whether by phone, card, letter, e-mail, or visit. General, automated, non-specific stuff will not have the impact or make the connection you need to encourage that prospect to pick up the phone when the time comes. Sometimes there's no substitute for a hand-written note - it takes about five minutes of your time and you'd be amazed that impact it has on the recipient. sometimes a mix of media is appropriate, depending on the volume you need it to cover every week or the type of sale. The only constant you can count on is that if you don't do it, your sale with go to the guy who does. Sometimes its trial and error, but you have to use common sense, especially having to do with timing and frequency. You really don't want to overdo it - an e-mail every other day is likely overkill . . .

Consistency, reliability and accountability are the keys to good sales practice, and the follow-up should be part of that - if the customer feels you'll be there before the sale, think how much they'll appreciate you being there after the sale.

CEOs ARE Different!

There have been several entries on these pages about reaching the "C" Suite or the CEO with your business to business marketing efforts. Why all the hoopla about a title selection on your list data card? Research shows that CEOs are a special breed of cat, and need to be approached in a different way than other managers or directors.

In-depth analysis of interviews with over 200 CEOs in the early part of this century shows that there are several traits that these captains of industry have in common (no, this isn't a conspiracy theory, just a little science thrown into the art). CEOs interviewed were almost universally labeled "decisive" when asked to pick a trait that most described their leadership style. These are clearly take-charge kinda guys, and that personality type has little tolerance or time for long, detailed, involved explanations of complex features or touchy-feely analogies - "just the facts, ma'am", and I'll decide based on that. If there was ever a group to which you want to pitch cold, hard benefits, this is it.

That same research revealed a reluctance to collaborate on some types of actions or decisions, or at least seeking the counsel of a limited few - the captain of the ship doesn't ask the deck hand which way to steer. They work in committees reluctantly, but are quick to form task forces and committees under them on order to receive varied input summarized from the group's spokesman. That funnel gets very narrow at the top. Your chances of getting an "Upward" referral from your awareness campaign or from a pass-along of your direct marketing are low indeed - these guys kick the knowledge down, not pull from below, at least not directly.

So knowing that they keep their own counsel, and that they make decisions fast based on facts, how do you reach them? That same research showed that they are still vulnerable to some of the normal emotional approaches, like envy, or fear of losing, either opportunity or missing knowledge. These folks like to be the first to know, and they like the finer things because they've earned them. Luxury goods have a great chance of reaching the "C" suite by marketing at events and activities that cater to them - golf tournaments, exotic car races, art auctions, private gatherings for charities, polo matches, tennis matches, and horse races that are nationally televised. There are many others, but the idea is to attach your brand to the event, and to have others there who represent the brand through use - you see six older gentlemen in a hospitality tent all wearing the same shoes or watch, you'll get the idea how powerful this can be.

What media works best? Unfortunately, it's my old favorite, "It Depends". Social media is likely not a good choice - this is an older group, although occasionally their wives (this group as a whole is overwhelmingly male unless otherwise specified) will buy them gifts or make a recommendation. Print media works well if selected carefully - *WSJ*, *Robb Report*, *GQ*, *New Yorker*, *NYT*, are all reasonable choices. Mail works well but has to work its way through several gatekeepers to get there, and if not carefully executed, may not ever get there. Dimensional mail works very well if executed properly, just don't get too clever, they don't have the time to work to figure out the inside joke. TV, forget it, they don't have time. Radio, lots of leakage and only a few stations nationally that make sense, mostly talk or news formats. Syndicated programs work better, but steer clear of politically-oriented programming - these guys pride themselves on making independent decisions based on facts, not on someone else's rhetoric.

Sometimes a purely demographic approach will be effective - the average CEO is 60 years old, an independent thinker, male, white, and Christian. They own 2.5 houses on average, 5.5 vehicles, and are married*. They are extremely busy, have little free time and want to enjoy what time they have to the fullest. Sponsorships and partnerships can be effective if you select a partner whose brand aligns well with yours. Personal recommendations and referrals really carry the day here, so treating your customers with extremely high levels of service, extreme discretion bordering on secrecy, and over-super serve them so that they make referrals proudly, you can bet the word will spread.

Just understanding that this group is different is a great start, and respecting them as such is a step in the right direction. Facts, accuracy, discretion are watch words for reaching this elusive group, it's tough but not impossible!

*based on corporate census data from *Fortune* magazine

Face-To-Face Works Best

If you're a small business owner or manager, you've probably been focused on new customer acquisition for the last year or so, just trying to survive. You've probably tried and tested numerous methods of "getting the word out" in your local business community, using supposedly "tried and true" methods, like publication advertising, fliers in public places, trade shows, maybe e-mail campaigns, social media promotions, maybe some direct mail, coupon packs, maybe even radio or other types of mass media. If you're like most we've worked with in this situation, the results from these efforts were mixed at best.

What most of these types of promotions lack is brand recognition in the local community, and lack of focus, either geographically or psychographically, being off message or appearing in the wrong place to the wrong audience.

Even in this day and age of technology and social networking, the most effective method we've found to initiate and foster working, professional relationships is fact-to-face networking. More information about you and your business, your integrity, your honestly, your competence and capability can be transmitted in a fifteen minute conversation at a business mixer than in a YouTube video, a Facebook profile, a LinkedIn resume, a brochure or direct mailer.

Professional business networking is a conversation with a point. I'm not talking about those business card pass out fests, where you're only goal is to gab and grab as many cards as you can and get out. I'm talking about educational, informative, honest conversations in a low-pressure, conducive environment, where real professionals can find out about each other's businesses, get a sense of their goals, approach and vision, where you can gauge their position in the professional landscape, maybe meet some of their colleagues, watch how they interact with others.

It's an art form, and resembles dating in many ways. You're looking for common ground, common experiences, common approaches or beliefs, that you can use to base an ongoing relationship upon. You're looking for people to whom you'd trust your business, one you've worked hard to build, and you want to be careful with that particular property.

Of course, there are limitations - you can only be in so many places at once, and you can only meet so many people in a given hour. But it's not quantity you're focused on here, its quality. There are some numbers involved, but they are less daunting than you might believe. For example, if you go to four events a month, one a week on average, you can probably meet 15-20 people a month. Of those, maybe 50% are worth keeping in touch with or fostering, for various reasons (they're a competitor, there's never any need for your service, they're not senior enough to be decision maker yet, etc.). That's 120 new people a year, each of whom represents a business, a circle of friends, associates, colleagues, family, neighbors and other relatives, who probably total approximately 50. That's 6000 connections a year, every year, who now have access to you, if you've made the right impression on each of the initial contacts - meaning you haven't talked their ear off, wasted their time, have expressed a sincere interest in their business, asked meaningful questions, haven't said anything offensive, etc.

If half of those connections actually investigate further, and elect to do business with you, that's 3000 new customers a year. With an average order of $50, that's $150,000 a year off single-transaction new business alone, let alone referrals, repeat business, up-sell, and a host of other interactions. All for having a drink and a chat once a week. Not too shabby.

Face-to-face interactions allow you to be you, and represent your business in a way that no other media or method allows. Making the connections is only half the battle, following up and nurturing those relationships, keeping them fresh and active is another story altogether.

Go forth and network, and you don't even need an Internet connection!

What Salespeople Want Prospects and Clients to Know

(An open letter from Salespeople the world over to clients and prospects)

Dear Prospect,

As an ethical, professional, courteous sales person, there are some things I repeatedly encounter when interacting with clients and prospects that cause me some concern, and I think with a little education we can clear them up and interact on a more effective and profitable basis.

1) I'm not trying to trick you, steal from you, or talk you into something that you don't want or need. I'm a professional, and as such, know that it's much more productive and profitable for me to keep long-term clients than it is to turn and burn a host of one-time victims. I thrive on repeat business, and the last thing I want to do is pull a fast one on you or take advantage of you.

2) The more you tell me, the better I can help you achieve your goals. You wouldn't lie to or withhold information from your attorney, and you shouldn't be lying to or holding out on your accountant, so why do you feel you need to be guarded in your conversations with me? Are you afraid if I learn something I'll use it to talk you into buying more? I'd rather solve your complete problem right the first time, so you'll refer me to your friends.

3) I talk to people all day long for a living, often about problems similar to yours. I *might* have picked up a thing or two from those conversations, and that makes my knowledge more complete and recent than yours is likely to be. That knowledge deserves some respect.

4) Just because you *think* you can't afford what I have to offer at the moment, doesn't mean it's a waste of my time to get to know you and your challenges. Take the meeting anyway, you might be surprised at what you learn, and at how I can help you no matter what your budget. Maybe not right this second, but at some point along the way.

5) The more you trust me, and the better and reciprocal our relationship becomes, the more value *you* derive from it. Salespeople are out on the streets all day learning and solving problems in creative ways. I know things that might

be of help, at no cost to you, if you just give me a try. The risk is really minimal, and the return can be tremendous.

6) I have an ethical obligation to keep your private and corporate information to myself. I also have an ulterior motive to do so. I won't last long if I go around blabbing client info to other clients, will I? I'm a professional, in it for the long haul, and keeping quiet serves any number of purposes.

7) You won't hurt my feelings by calling and telling me you bought from someone else. As a professional with some experience, I've developed a pretty thick skin, so don't worry about my reaction, I can assure you it will be professional and appropriate. Please have the courtesy to return follow-up calls, don't just let them go to voicemail and ignore them, hoping I'll get the message - it's rude and counterproductive.

8) We can all use a hand once in a while. If I've done a great job, tell me so, and then tell two colleagues who can also buy from us as well. That's the *real* currency salespeople live off of, referrals. It takes thirty seconds, is painless and free, and would really make my world better.

9) The reverse is also true: if I screw up, please tell me quickly so we can fix the problem, get a solution worked out, patch things up and move on. Don't let those issues fester and then just stop returning calls for no apparent reason - it's not healthy.

10) I'm just as anxious to solve your problem as you are to get it solved. The sooner we stop dancing and start producing, the faster we'll both get where we're going. I'll be happy to answer any questions for your superiors, cover your behind, make it right, do whatever is required to protect our relationship, so stop worrying about it and start fixing it sooner rather than later.

Hope you find this helpful in our interactions in the future. I think you'll find if you keep these things in mind, you'll get more of what you want, at lower cost, faster, and with greater enthusiasm all around. Be the hero of your own situation, and help me help you!

Sincerely,
Joe Salesperson

Chapter Takeaways:

1. The Sales department at many organizations is operating at odds with the Marketing department and this ongoing battle creates more than disharmony, it dilutes the efforts of both and reduces productivity and profitability. The two entities need to work in coordinated, synchronous fashion. The ways to bridge the gap are varied and myriad, but it usually boils down to common vision, common goal, and good communication of need and function between the two.

2. Sales is about creating expectations, developing relationships between the brand and the customer, and living up to those expectations and exceeding them. Under-promise and over-deliver is a good place to start and a mantra of many successful sales organizations.

3. Sales is also an art best practiced by the most experienced professionals with years of training and perspective, good people skills and a vast well of knowledge to dip into to drive prospects into the purchase decision using a mix of logic, emotion and knowledge of human psychology.

4) Branding

Top Talent Will Out

I recently received an e-mail promotion for Disney Institute corporate training and executive growth coaching - called "D-Thinking Your Organization." In keeping with the Disney brand of old, it's professional, well-done, creative, and deceptively simple. It shows an image of two executives (presumably) with large cardboard cartons on their head, sort of sparring in the hallway - ostensibly thinking "inside-the-box."

Disney execs have long been revered for their creativity and resourcefulness, and more importantly for instilling the company culture in their employees so deeply that it affects the rest of their lives in a very positive way. I've seen a couple of them speak and it's mesmerizing to hear their stories of how their customer-oriented service-excessive culture affects the lives of employees and customers alike. Tremendous stories abound of how good-will on the part of one person in a very minor role in the company affects a customer in a profound way to the point where the customer becomes an eternal evangelists for the brand. This is the nirvana all brand managers seek, and they have found it, achieved it, and kept it alive after the loss of the founder many years ago.

The point is that the e-mail promotion, a medium that many so-called marketing gurus have determined is of limited value for corporate marketing due to saturation of the audience, lack of permanence, and a host of other reasons, worked - it reached a potential customer, a qualified prospect (me), and got my attention to the point where I not only read the whole thing, but studied the image, analyzed the copy and the headline, and filed it rather than deleting it. So much for gurus.

The Disney brand extends to every facet of their business, and promotion is no exception. They always manage to be tasteful, honest, transparent, and relevant, while being effective in showing their creativity and expertise, in subtle, understated ways. When they undertake something, it's done RIGHT. Occasionally that means they're a little behind the curve in terms of time or adoption of technology, but when they get there, all the bugs are worked out, they maximize the medium's potential, and put it to best use for their purposes. Kudos.

Do Your Clients Know You, or Just What You've Reminded Them Of Recently?

Service businesses are funny things sometimes. Clients tend to pigeonhole your service firm based on what service you first performed for them. They rarely actually read the literature you leave behind, especially if it's a referral, and they usually don't go back and search it when another type of job arises, no matter how closely related to the first. So your first impression, your first engagement and your referrals tend to shape your brand for you in the customer's mind, unless you steer it, expand it and broaden it on an almost continual basis.

It's an easy trap to fall into, especially for smaller firms, who may appear more limited than they are. I'm no exception to this unfortunately, although I try to avoid it if I can. I have one customer who only thinks of me in connection with trade show displays, because that was the first part of a multi-faceted strategy we recommended for them when entering into a new vertical market. Not that she doesn't KNOW we offer a full range of marketing services, from strategic planning to campaign execution and executive guidance, it's just that I don't reside in that part of her brain and I'm not connected to her other needs in a way that immediately comes to mind when they arise - I have to make a concerted effort to "remind" her that we are a full-service firm, so that we get connected in that way.

How many of your customers or internal clients only think of you when they need or have a question about a very narrow range of elements, the one you did for them last, or first? It's something you might want to explore, and you can test it pretty easily: Call them up and ask "Do you know that we also offer . . ." and see what the response is. Call under the auspices of keeping in touch, a good thing regardless, but hunt for that specific piece of data during the conversation. You might be surprised by the result.

It may seem strange, but that's just how the brain works - humans learned to survive by recognizing and remembering patterns, and noticing anything that breaks the pattern, like sensing movement in the brush created by a prey animal. Once a pattern is established, a la` your firm performing a certain service, that pattern is retained and it's difficult to change that perception.

Here's the fix: broaden your marketing efforts. Don't go against brand, in fact, if you're a multi-service firm, this will strengthen that tenet of your brand. But highlight a different angle, a different aspect or subgroup of your offerings in a series of marketing launches - it's like baiting a fishing line with different baits at different parts of the line - you increase the odds of catching something from the same pond. Even if you think you only offer one thing, and one of your brand characteristics is that you do one thing and do it the best of anyone, there are still different angles and facets of that "one thing" that you can use to "bait the hook" with. Try it, see if you don't get the phone ringing with new business from old clients who "Didn't know you offered that."

Self-Branding At Its Finest

Your own name plays a huge part of your personal brand, but how many of us really get to determine that element and as an adult actually go through with it? Apparently, if you're in a gang in Baltimore and likely elsewhere, you get that chance, and sometimes it can backfire!

According to an article in the *Baltimore Sun*, gangbangers all have nicknames, ones that are so ubiquitous, that they are actually used in court filings! Unfortunately, the thought given to what that nickname is might be a bit lacking and can come back to haunt them when they get into the "System."

Imagine being the defense lawyer trying to convince a jury of your client's innocence on a murder or assault charge when the young man sitting at your side has "Murder" tattooed on his neck for all to see, or is questioned by the prosecution and addressed by his nickname, "Bloody Dog" multiple times into the court record and read back repeatedly. Good luck with that . . .

In their world, picking a scary sounding nickname gives you a certain amount of street credibility, and often tells something about you, just as any brand should. Unfortunately, that brand is designed for a very specific audience, and has a negative impact on those outside that audience. We'll call these two-way brands, like a two-way mirror. One side reflects the owner's identity to this group, the other side reflects a starkly different image – one to be avoided at all costs.

Some commercial brands are two-ways as well, and this is usually a result of faulty or lack of consumer research when crafting the original identity. Brands that reflect too much of an "inside" perspective are built for insiders and those "outside" the circle just don't "Get it." Not a very good way to attract new customers, or even to spark curiosity - once you investigate the odd name that doesn't resonate, discover it has nothing to do with anything you're interested in, you ignore it, discount it, or avoid it altogether. Ford had to live down early 1900s labels of Fix Or Repair Daily, and Found On Road – Dead, in the early days of the company branding effort.

Another that comes to mind is "Go Daddy." The company created that brand from an internal meeting of some kind and simply forced recognition through effective creative advertising on a huge scale. But if you just mentioned the name prior to that, it certainly doesn't sound like a domain name registration company - there are no reliable attributes that the words "Go Daddy" together evoke. Certainly they don't bring to mind orderliness, convenience, permanence, cooperation, creativity, or any of a number of other characteristics that by definition such a company would embody. Yet, it's a fast-growing company with high financial performance and a good chunk of market share - not bad for an upstart with a quirky brand . . .!

Your personal brand reflects the characteristics you want the public to see, regardless of who that public is. Every adult has the opportunity to create a personal brand, and can have their name legally changed with a simple hearing by a judge and some basic paperwork - as long as the reason has nothing to do with your need to evade the law or debt of any kind, have at it. Entertainers do it all the time - would you tune in to watch Larry Zeiger interview celebrities? But before retirement, Larry King pulled in the occasional viewer on a regular basis. Go figure.

Some internal reflection is in order when choosing your personal brand. Give it some thought, understand that it has to be viewed by the world at large and have some meaning, then back up the moniker with the attributes you hold in highest regard, consistently. Now you're talking branding . . .

Effective Branding Awards - Winner Announced

I'm always in search of particularly effective branding efforts, just to enjoy a job well-done. Knowing how hard it is to carry out brand development on a daily basis, and how important the initial thinking is in spring-boarding the brand forward, I'm always looking for those that put in the effort up front and got it right.

This week's winner is Geek Squad, the computer service firm that operates out of Best Buy stores. These guys thought about EVERYTHING, and live the brand every day. I've had the opportunity to try these guys out several times in the last year, and they are nothing if not consistent.

Each technician is called an "Officer," and they always come in full uniform, including a badge and ID card, and arrive in a branded car, usually a white Volkswagen Beetle with black fenders and the logo on the doors - further reinforcing the quasi-police image. Their delivery is rather police-like, definitely gentle, but no-nonsense, they are extremely respectful of the customer's home and work-space, touching as little as possible, asking few questions that are not directly related to the job at hand, and get right to work. They solve the problem or make a recommendation to repair at more extensive facilities or replace the machine, they come armed with a full bevy of software diagnostic tools, all branded, and get the job done, transact payment, and disappear to the next jobsite.

There was so little variation in my three experiences it was spooky, like I said; these guys are consistent. Given the labor pool from which the company draws for this position and the human factors that have to be accommodated in any national company, I'm still astounded how well they carry the brand. I know when I see those little cars on the road that they're on their way to help some other poor computer-illiterate victim of the diabolic black box, and the feeling associated with the brand is always extremely positive.

They set out with a good idea, they went full tilt toward fleshing it out, and they train the employees to clearly live and transmit the brand effectively with EVERY interaction.

Brand Effectiveness Key to Membership Growth

The visibility, awareness, and effectiveness of your organization's brand directly impact your ability to recruit and retain members. If your organization isn't the first thing member prospects think of when they turn to industry issues, there's work to be done.

But where to start?

As popular wisdom has it, knowing and admitting you have a problem is half way to solving it. In this case, that means doing a little member research to determine how your members and prospective members view your organization through its brand. This can take one of several forms, including a quick poll on your website, a phone survey, an e-mail or electronic survey, or a paper/mail survey. Regardless of the format, the recipient list should be equal parts members and prospects, to get both perspectives and spot any disconnects between those that know the organization from the inside versus what the brand alone presents to the outside world. The included questions should be formulated so that the responses returned are actionable, and give you some indication of their perceptions of the brand and the organization behind it, based on their actual experience with you, as customers, as members, as industry participants.

Reading the results in a timely fashion is important, as the cyclic nature of nonprofit schedules creates peaks and valleys in the brand perception and awareness level, depending upon what time of the year it is, and how high the level of activity involving members is at the time you launch the survey. For organizations that have even more volatile years, it may be necessary to do two sets of surveys at different times of the year and compare the results to get a good reliable read on the level of awareness you can count on.

The results of your survey are one source of data, but there are other sources that, while less formal or quantifiable, are just as valid in getting a read on your brand awareness and effectiveness. These include interviews with board members, committee members, volunteers, chapter presidents or directors, vendors, other related professionals, including members of related associations, and members of ASAE.

Once all this data is collected, it needs to be interpreted accurately so that the actions you take drive your brand efforts in the most effective direction possible. Some items will be readily apparent if the surveys and interviews were constructed correctly. One good tool you can use to read your results is to retrieve the set of brand characteristics from the marketing archives, and see how many of your responses line up with those characteristics. If your responses, including the open-ended comments, use some of the terms and attributes that make up your organization's brand, then you've got a good solid start on reading your data correctly and rating a good score on your brand effectiveness. Conversely, if very few or none of the responses include those attributes on the list, there's a good chance there's a disconnect between what you're trying to convey with your brand, and how it's being perceived by the various populations it's designed to serve.

Now that you've got a read on how well you're doing, how do you go about improving? The answer, much as it's been overused by too many of us in today's litigious society – "it depends." It depends upon what your data tells you, and every case is different. However there are some common scenarios and a few valuable remedies to match them.

Scenario #1 – Our brand registers very low on the surveys for memorability. Typically this means that your customer base doesn't remember your brand in response to a question designed to illicit a favorable response unprompted. Your organization isn't top of mind for them as relates to your products or services, and someone else's brand is. That could mean that your exposure frequency is too low, or they don't see enough from you to keep memorability high enough. It could be that a competitor has captured some key emotional connection to the customer that you have not, despite an inferior product or service – they're not as good, but customers remember them because they're "out there" more. This can be remedied with some increase in exposure to key audiences – your top buyers should hear more from you in a positive light to reassure them that you offer the product or services that give the best value. Putting your brand in front of them for positive reasons, like a price discount, a new offer that really saves money, rebate eligibility or other product or service related reason other than to sell them something should go a long way toward remedying this issue. It will boost memorability without seeming like you're overselling them; a positive cognitive light that will cement the brand in the uppermost memory of the customer.

Scenario #2 – Our brand rates favorably and has high memory retention among customers, but neither do as well among prospects.

Usually, this indicates that your product or service has to be "seen to be believed" – its value is best seen at delivery or in the transaction, rather than prior to receiving it. This is a sticky problem that has to do as much with promotional direction and relevance as anything else. Your customers know you and have experienced your value, been satisfied with the product or service upon and after delivery and the reputation of the brand was reinforced positively. Prospects, on the other hand, only know you by your "public" face – advertising, packaging, direct marketing, and sponsorship associations. The brand unfortunately has little carriage by word of mouth, based on the fact that satisfied customers are not waving your flag and passing on the good word to prospects themselves. Prospects only get a read based on what you tell them. Look to your research and find those key hot buttons of your best customers, and promote those attributes to prospects more heavily. Also, compare your reading on prospects versus customers in other areas of your brand – you may find another disconnect in their perceptions that could cause this effect, and you can remedy both with a shift in your promotional or creative approach to highlight those key elements more heavily. Align your creative with those highest ranking attributes of your best customers, and the prospects should get the best, most relevant perception of your product.

These are just two of the possible outcomes to this type of analysis. In Part II, we'll outline some additional outcomes and the directions they indicate you should make adjustments. Suffice to say that, if you're brand is aligned with your message and your audience, you've got a strong package for success.

Brand Effectiveness Key to Membership Growth, Part II

Previously, we discussed using in-depth member survey work to boost the visibility, awareness and effectiveness of your organization's brand, and how it can directly impact your ability to recruit and retain members. If your organization isn't the first thing member prospects think of when they turn to industry issues, there's work to be done.

Your survey may provide mixed results that don't show a clear direction. Often this is an indication that there is a disconnect between the brand you put out to the external world, and the one you use to craft the questions! That alone tells you something, and a series of follow-up interviews with the same basic set of queries to the external and internal groups should help clear up the discrepancy.

Other sources of data can help you check your brand effectiveness as well. Interviews with those alternate stake holders should be couched slightly differently, and can use more "insider jargon" in the questions, as their awareness starts off at a higher level. They can give you a median read, between the internal and the external, and this can often help you reconcile the disparate results mentioned above.

Take Stock

An inventory can be helpful in analyzing your brand's effectiveness. Simply create a list of all the places where your brand appears, in what context, what medium, attached to what product, message or outreach vehicle, and see if they seem to have an obvious pattern, if they are aligned. Often pulling samples from the archives and lining them all up together can be very enlightening. You may be unaware of a brand shift that may have occurred over time, small miscues that send a less the consolidated message to the recipient. One example of this is when an outsource vendor or contractor uses your brand in their program, and it doesn't match your normal set of brand characteristics. If you are seen as a very sophisticated, august and professionally ethical branded organization, and an outsider puts your logo as a sponsor on a ticket giveaway coupon for a concert, which would be a brand slip or miscue. If several of these items have crept into your inventory, it may be time to put some tighter controls on the use of your brand, and provide some increased education within the organization about the importance of protecting the brand and how to use it properly.

Top of Mind

Keeping memorability high is another positive effect of a well -aligned and effective brand. If your brand is consistent with individual experience, that experience will be more memorable. L.L. Bean shows a great example of this. Their "Return any time, no questions asked" return policy has been with them since virtually the beginning of the company. They were so confident in the quality of their products, they couldn't dream of anyone sending them back, and thus the perceived risk of such a policy was low. That policy became part of their brand, and is now a deeply embedded positive characteristic, so much so that there was near revolt when a senior staffer proposed eliminating it to help save money. As it turns out, their return rate is notably lower than their competitors, and the savings realized would have been more than offset by the damage to their brand as a trusted, honorable retailer of fine outdoor merchandise. As a result, when you get an L. L. Bean catalog in the mail, you instantly put in the back of your mind that the purchase from there is of lower risk, and therefore a greater possibility, as a result of that policy. That gives them a competitive advantage, and keeps their customer retention high and their loyalty even higher, due to the memorability of that policy.

Brands Aren't Built In A Day

If you've launched a new product, are a new organization or subgroup within a larger organization, you know the difficulty of setting the stage for a lasting brand. It takes many, many customer touches to build a brand effectively, and with non-profit, member driven organizations, the rate of touch is often affected by budgetary constraints. That puts the building process on the slow track, as the mailings, e-mails, directories, guides, meetings and other activities slowly mount up in the member's mind. Each piece of the building process must be consistent, and have relevance and meaning for the recipient, or you undo much of the positive work up until then. Be patient. It can take years for an organization to reach a highly memorable, effective state with its brand, and many a good program has been discontinued by impatient senior staffers with a more cautious eye on the bottom line than knowledge of the branding process and its benefits.

If your brand message aligns with expectations, your touch rate is predictable and rising, and your organization has shown relevance for the audience it wishes to serve, you're on your way to a highly effective brand.

Ten Ways to Make Sponsorship Build Credibility, Visibility for Your Brand

Every business out there has probably been approached about a sponsorship, or included sponsorship in their marketing mix in one form or another, especially those with a consumer sales focus. But how do you make the selection of which one's might be the most effective long-term?

Careful selection of the events, products, and people you sponsor will allow you to activate that sponsorship to benefit fully from your association. In order to make a beneficial selection, you have to know your brand inside and out, and have a good handle on some of the more "outlying" characteristics that consumers have pinned to it – not just the ones you're broadcasting about it. Some of those alternative characteristics can make for very solid sponsorships if you pick them carefully and engage fully with all the opportunities they offer.

Many businesses don't engage fully with the opportunities they do select, and get less-than-optimal returns as a result. This is one situation where you really do get out what you put in. Don't stop at the logo on the sign, that's just the beginning. Here's ten ways to maximize the return on a sponsorship opportunity, planned or impromptu:

For Event Sponsorships:

10) **Make sure to provide adequate materials to the event hosts so that all participants receive something from you at the event.** Don't short the count on the collateral, the promotional items or the literature, because that one person who gets left out will carry that impression longer and to more people than all the rest combined.

9) **Be sure your brand is represented adequately, accurately and repeatedly.** You've purchased a certain level of exposure, and most event organizers will bend over backward to help you get it, but if you don't speak up and remind them, you may not get everything you were promised. Check everything to be sure the brand is represented in the best possible light, and that

it's reproduced at an adequate size, color fidelity and resolution to do you some good – after all, you paid for it.

8) Even if you don't have something already created, make sure you take advantage of every portion of the sponsorship package. Most sponsorships are multi-faceted, and usually multi-media. If you don't have elements in use already for each medium, be it flash video, print collateral, sales sheets, logo files in every possible format, bios, soundbites, banner ads, animated gifs, promotional blurbs and items, signage, banners, and other typical elements to take advantage of the whole package of opportunities, create whatever it is you're missing. You might be the only one of the sponsors who does, in which case, guess who's going to be the most memorable?

7) Make sure the audience matches your efforts. Most brands have a broad range of demographic, psychographic and geographic audiences it serves. Be sure the sponsorship you pick reaches at least a viable, sizeable niche slice of your total target market. If not, it doesn't make sense to participate.

6) Make your selection based on LIFETIME CUSTOMER VALUE, and not just acquisition cost. It may cost you $25 to reach, influence and close a new customer to buy your product once. But if the event sponsorship is a valid one, you not only close one sale, but in most cases (if you're doing your retention efforts correctly), you've gained a long-term customer who will enact or refer multiple sales over the next few years. Once you factor that in, the numbers on Return on Investment (ROI) work much better.

5) Do your part of participate in the success of the event. Your name and your brand is now attached to this event. Do you part to promote it, get some mileage of your own out of your participation, fill the stands and pack the seats – it's to your benefit, it drives that many more people to view your participation, and bring you more customers.

4) If the package doesn't fit, ask for what you want. Most event organizers want the sponsorship to benefit you, so that you'll repeat or extend your participation and become an evangelist for their event. They want to make you happy, and will negotiate in good faith if you have an alternative proposal to present. If you don't ask, they won't likely offer what you want. The tough part is accepting and using the valuations attached to each element. Most often it pays to just make the best overall deal you can, and work it to the fullest.

3) Pick events that make interaction logical. A mountain bike company sponsoring a swimming event doesn't make a lot of sense, but that same company sponsoring an off-road bike race makes perfect sense. That's not to say that you can't sponsor an event outside your industry, you just have to be selective so that the audience can easily make the connection between your brand and the activity they're engaged in at the moment.

2) Make the sponsorship an integral part of your strategy, even if it isn't. Plan your sponsorships to work with your product's sales curve, either to boost the top or fill in the troughs, seasonally or geographically. If you're expanding your service or delivery area, work events on the fringes of your current area to make the expansion more organic. If you sell primarily in the summer, work the earlier and earlier events, or later into the fall to extend your season and broaden your exposure.

1) Don't select more sponsorships or pick more events than you can fully support. The up-front cost is just the tip of the iceberg, and once you add manpower hours, staff training, brand monitoring time, collateral and participation costs, and follow-up and activation costs, it's easy to get over-extended, and not give a full effort to anything, a recipe for failure. Make an honest commitment to the right mix of events and participate fully for the greatest benefit.

Making smart selections when choosing a sponsorship is a combination of art and science, and the basis is really knowing your market, knowing your brand intimately, and using some common sense with an audience perspective. Sponsorship can be a strong part of your marketing mix, if you make the right choices and work them to the fullest.

Rebranding Your Organization – Change Management at Its Finest

Imagine your future: Your brand identity has been in place unchanged since the organization was founded in the 1950s; the marketplace has shifted; your brand characteristics are diffuse and have drifted and meandered virtually unguided for decades; your organization offers different benefits than it used to, because that's what the membership has dictated; and the membership base has shifted away from the traditional manufacturers and service suppliers to a full range of peripheral industries around a few core large members. It's time to rebrand! Now what?

Rebranding can offer your organization many things, almost all of them good. But to take advantage of them, you have to actively and proactively manage the change process. To do that, it all starts with research, planning, education and communication within your organization, almost all of it between your marketing department and the executive staff.

Start at the Top

Getting good data is key to making good decisions – that's an axiom that few can argue with, but that very few organizations take to heart when making strategic decisions. Rebranding is a very strategic decision, so in order to do it with the greatest positive impact, some critical research is in order. A good, old-fashioned Strengths, Weaknesses, Opportunities and Threats (SWOT) analysis will lead you down the right road in almost all instances if done honestly and thoroughly, with a little imagination thrown in.

Knowing your members' needs, desires and concerns is also critical – it's their club after all, and without them there is no need to have a brand at all! If you have a stranglehold on what role your organization plays in their personal or professional lives, you're a good way toward the goal of crafting an effective new brand around that group of members.

Knowing where your organization stands in the competitive spectrum in their professional lives, and what goods and services they turn to you for, puts you even further down the right road. Ask the tough questions – if you can use a rebranding to jettison unsuccessful programs because your research shows that no one uses that program or doesn't think of you as offering that, you form a tighter brand identity, and create an opportunity to offer something similar but better later.

The last piece of research should be to hunt for similar or related brands in your own and other related industries. If the one you want to use is taken, you need to know that before you get too far down the path, to avoid infringement of trademark problems later.

Create a Plan

Rebranding is an organization-wide event and it touches everyone in the organization to one degree or another. Some elements will take longer to prepare than others, so your action priorities should be ordered upon implementation times and logistic concerns, so that all the pieces come together at a specific point in time at the end. You'll want to launch the new brand in a short, intense period of activity, to discourage backsliding and create impact. Some groups have tried to sneak the new brand in under the radar, with no fanfare or celebration. Those types of soft launches usually take longer to enter and become retained in the public consciousness among your audience, and ultimately cost your organization time, money and credibility.

Derive a set of newly-generated brand characteristics from your member research, and task your marketing department to create a summary statement describing the new brand in those terms. Use that statement to graphically craft a representation of its meaning and create the new brand. If done properly, it will carry all the critical information and translate those characteristics into an image that communicates them clearly. Your plan should map out these steps and give a rationale for each of them that makes concrete sense to the internal audience. That plan is the basis for your communication both internally and externally.

TEST, Test, Test

Most organizations don't get it right on the first try. And most don't know they've got it wrong until it's too late, because they don't test. Internal and external reviews, focus groups and first-hand interviews will give you tremendous insight as to the accuracy of the image in projecting your brand's characteristics, and will give you insight as to the level and speed of acceptance you can expect among your target audience. If you meet with resistance, or it's not memorable, or not accurate, you can waste precious resources trying to correct it later. Research is relatively cheap insurance against launching a poorly-crafted new brand. Done correctly, it can give you the confidence to launch the new brand with pride and have it met with predictable success. This type of research has some nuances to it, and many organizations don't have the specialized knowledge and skill sets on staff to do it justice. For them it makes good financial sense to hire out to the experts for this portion. Most cities have a selection of reliable research firms that would be happy to help you launch your new brand correctly.

Communicate, Early and Often

Once you have what you feel is the definitive brand identity nailed down, a little preliminary education is in order. The mantra that good public speakers and presenters follow will work well here as well: "Tell them what you're going to say, say it, and then tell them what you said." That first step, the advance alert is important, so that there is some warning, and the launch isn't completely cold. It lets the audience know that there's a change coming and they can brace for it. It gives you a chance to set the stage, set expectations and show a little of your rationale behind the change, show the advantages it offers and show the benefits of the change in a positive light. The better you prepare the audience, the faster your adoption curve will evolve, and the higher your acceptance level will be – and that saves you time and money. The more easily they accept the new identity, the less time and money you have to spend to convince them.

Repetition and consistency are two great keys to success. The more places they audience sees that new brand, and the more consistent that presentation is, the higher your acceptance will be. The repetition is largely a budgetary issue, but Operations needs to get in on the game here too. As part of your planning, you should have conducted a brand inventory, showing each and every instance where your brand appears and in what context. Pull out that inventory and review it now, so you can arrange the list of changes in priority order. The highest time priority should be awarded to the most visible instances, the places with the highest volume and widest impact. Letterheads, envelopes, business cards, forms, newsletters and other items that number in the tens of thousands used per year, and distributed in large numbers on a regular basis should come first, as those will give you the highest penetration for the dollar. Items like shipping crate stencils, and the sign on the building can come a bit later. Fax cover sheets, e-mail signatures, and meeting signs are often overlooked initially, but those are fairly high-priority items. Brochures, membership kits and the like, while produced in high numbers, aren't distributed in high numbers, and have relatively low impact initially. Websites, blogs etc. change instantly (virtually) and should be high on the list as they are often the destination for many of your other marketing efforts. Take the ego out of your decision-making and use impact sphere to guide your priority decisions.

Out With The Bad, In With The Good

One of the resistance points you'll likely encounter is the so-called "waste" that goes along with a rebranding. Backsliding and phasing in the new brand as supplies run low or out will slow adoption and give mixed impressions to the audience. Make a clean break, and dump everything that carries the old brand – don't use it. Part of your planning and communication process should have been to influence decisions by those who resupply the organization, to help minimize waste. In the long term, getting rid of the 22 leftover tradeshow tchotchkes with the old brand on them isn't really a waste if it prevents a diluted message from being transmitted to your audience. Example: Hershey's new label was phased in (old label supplies were NOT pulled from the shelves) – that worked, but ONLY because the brand was imprinted so well – cereal brands usually do not fare as well. When in doubt, dump it all!

Timing Is Key

The decision on the timing of the new launch will differ from group to group, but one tried-and-true solution is to use the Annual Convention or other major meeting as a platform to launch the new brand. This type of timing gives you more bang for your marketing buck, and allows you to reach a greater percentage of your intended audience at once, in a controlled environment over a limited time span. It forces you to hit deadlines, to create a definitive point of impact and allows you to create the kind of repetition and consistency required to make this effort work.

Do The Paperwork

Don't forget to record the date of first use for your new brand, you'll need it for your new trademark application, which of course you've been preparing all along the way, to protect your new brand. File the initial paperwork as soon as the first use and three subsequent public uses can be shown. Launching at the Annual Meeting makes that easy, as the initial and other uses are all virtually concurrent, and you can show the quantities distributed and the reach of the new mark very easily.

Rebranding is a challenging process, but one that can drive all sorts of positive change throughout your organization. Handled thoroughly and thoughtfully, it can pay significant benefits in both the long and short term.

Brand Strength Assessment Tools You Can Use Now

Senior management at most successful businesses have realized that their brand, and the characteristics it represents, is one of the most valuable assets they own. If used properly, a powerful brand can propel a business' profitability for years to come, guide product development, enhance revenue in a variety of ways, and drive their business' growth. But how do you know if your brand is strong, if it is being diluted or damaged, or is entirely corrupt and even damaging?

Through work with a host of national companies and a wide variety of brands, I developed some tools we use to assess the strength of a brand, highlight potential weak spots, and reveal opportunities based on the results of some test questions. These were developed and vetted through one-to-one, lengthy interview research conducted over years, with customers of service, product, consumer and b-to-b purveyors. Each was refined and adjusted to meet the specific type of business, and then the data aligned along four quadrants using a multi-variant matrix to correct for industry and business model differences.

If answered honestly, these questions are structured to inform brand managers, marketing VPs, and senior management where things can be strengthened and where they can be capitalized upon for great effect. You can apply this same test (except for some proprietary differences) to your brand and do your own quick assessment. The more times you perform the test within your group of stakeholders, the more accurate it becomes, as more data points will tend to bring out strong linkages and commonalities within your organization. It can be segmented by department, to give you a read on how your brand info filters through various lenses internally based on job function. Or you can split it by job responsibility or title strata to determine whether your brand ideals have filtered down from the top or originate at the bottom.

Now the real question is, if you score below 40, what can you do to increase your score and strengthen your brand. At least some answers can be found in an analysis of the data from these questions as well. A follow-up article to this one coming next time will provide some insights as to how to use the data to get the job done quickly and cost-effectively. For now, on to the test:

Answer all 25 of the following questions in the following way.

- Assign a 1 if the answer is "Never"
- Assign a 2 if the answer is "Sometimes"
- Assign a 3 if the answer is "Almost Always"
- Assign a 4 if the answer is "Absolutely Always"

Total the responses and score your brand's power, integration and saturation based on these ranges:

- 25 - 40 - Brand is not well integrated and is vulnerable to pirating or may be damaged easily
- 41 - 55 – Brand needs support both internally and externally, not doing you as much good as it could be
- 56 - 75 – Brand is solid, but could use some polishing. Review with staff, add weight to priority scale
- 76 - 100 – Brand is strong. Lower end of scale (below 85) needs additional buffing; above 90, you could see through this company the brand is so well represented and transparent.

---

1. We actively investigate what is important to our customers, using research, face-to-face interviews, questionnaires, suggestion boxes, etc.

2. We understand how our customers feel about our products and services.

3. We judge the effectiveness of our brand in terms of how it looks and feels to our customers – not how it seems to us.

4. We understand the attitudes of our customers and their changing views and needs.

5. We don't have to discount prices in order to attract and keep our customers.

6. Our customers can state quite clearly and simply what is important about our brand to them, and why they think it is different.

7. Our communication plan includes all the various places and ways in which we interact with our customers.

8. We have aligned our organizational structure, operations and culture with our brand values.

9. We understand what differentiates our brand from our competitors.

10. Everyone in our organization knows what our brand stands for and can articulate that idea simply and clearly.

11. Everyone in our organization knows what they have to do to deliver on our brand promise.

12. Our communications, marketing, service delivery, finance and HR functions are all aligned with our brand objectives.

13. Branding is championed throughout our organization, from the CEO down.

14. Strengthening and protecting the company's brand is a fundamental driver behind our organization's long-term goals.

15. We have a brand management program in place that is continually looking for new and more effective ways to protect and enhance our brand throughout the organization.

16. Accounts quantifying the value of our brand to our business are included in our financial systems.

17. Details of our brand and the strategy that drives it are well documented and that information is available to those who need and desire it.

18. All key stakeholders are involved in our brand creation process.

19. Our company has systems in place for carefully monitoring the appropriateness, timeliness, integration and consistency of our branded communications.

20. We view brand as applying to far more than just our visual identity and our marketing communications.

21. Our brand includes not just our core organization but also our partners and key third party suppliers.

22. We regard our brand agency(ies) as our strategic partner(s) and actively involve them in organizational and communications planning and review sessions.

23. Our marketing and communications team have an integrated understanding of our brand and are in constant communication over brand-related activities and issues.

24. The consistency of our brand is paramount. It reaches way beyond just tactical brand campaigns and it is deeper than even key personnel changes.

25. If our brand did not exist, the vast majority of our customers would notice our absence and really miss having us in their lives.

Chapter Takeaways:

1. Brand-building is a critical element in any company's marketing efforts. It takes time, expense and effort, and careful stewardship of the brand brings strong positive benefits.

2. Sponsorship is a very well-respected brand building technique, but must be approached with thoughtfulness and respect, as it can easily do as much damage as good to the brand, and can easily drain extensive resources that could be spent with greater impact if the sponsorship has no activation vehicle.

3. You can test the health of your brand, and takes steps to rebuild or enhance the brand based on the test results.

5) Customer Service

Sometimes You Want To Go . . .Where Everybody Knows Your Name

Everybody wants to be wanted, or at least recognized. I have a few places where they know me on sight when I walk in the door, but that kind of permanence and stability has been rare, especially since I grew up outside the Nation's Capitol, where there are very few "natives" and the population is extremely transient. Too, I went to a very large university in Boston, where much of the student population was composed of commuters, so the typical school experience was very different, more focused on studying and less on social life, especially after dark, when a majority of the student body left for their own homes in the suburbs.

Business relationships are often like that, too: you meet, you greet, you follow up, maybe even work on a project or several, and then drift apart. Relationships like anything else have to be nurtured and tended to in order to survive and thrive. The relationship with your customers is just that way. It takes effort to nurture them and to keep customers aware of you and to keep your business top of mind.

Marketing can do that for you, but it must be sincere, and it must at least appear as much as possible to be PERSONAL. Your customers are humans, whether it's Business-to-Business or consumer market, and they deserve to be treated as such. Good marketing, especially direct mail copy, should appear to be written specifically to YOU. That DOESN'T mean you just use the word "you" a lot in the copy - there's an art to it, and if you're not feelin' the art, have a pro write your copy for you - it's worth it.

Customer service is often as simple as answering a question quickly and accurately. It can go as far as going above and beyond and addressing a long-standing problem and turning that complaining customer into an evangelist.

I was the recipient of some tremendous customer service recently, at a business networking mixer, at the Intercontinental Hotel in Baltimore. There is one place where they know me when I walk in the door, and this is it. Before I had gotten through the lobby into the bar proper, the top notch bartender, Elizabeth, had my "usual" beverage prepared for me, ready to go without me asking or even looking in her direction. Now, in reality, I have only been a guest there about six times in the last year, but it's always for the same event, the same time of day and the same day of the week, and our schedules collided on a regular basis - but she took the time and energy to remember after just a few small interactions who I was, what I looked like (winter and summer mind you, no identifying scarf or coat to help) what I liked to drink, and how I liked to get the evening started. Terrific! Kudos to Elizabeth for taking the initiative and providing outstanding service - and kudos to Arpad and the staff at the Intercontinental for realizing that sometimes employees need to be empowered to go above and beyond to REALLY please customers, and for allowing them the latitude to do it. I'm sure preparing a drink before the customer asks isn't in the InterContinental's policy book, but Elizabeth knew that I would be pleased and she was right.

Under-promise and Over-deliver - Tougher than it Sounds

I had a good customer service experience which I thought tied into my belief in customer service as marketing device. I've written several articles on the value of good customer service as a marketing tool, so when I run across an instance in real life that proves the theory, I like to recognize their efforts.

I drive a gas guzzling, over-huge SUV - since I don't commute regularly, my annual mileage is about 8,000 a year, about 1/3 of the national average. Unfortunately it has the same maintenance needs as if I drove it 20,000 miles a year - except for the frequency of things like tires, brakes, and other wearable parts, that still wear out on schedule, just my elongated version. In 2006, on vehicles that size, now on virtually all of them, the manufacturer installed special valve stems that have the ability to measure the tire pressure on each tire, and a sender to tell you what the pressure is on a continual basis. As you might expect, these little marvels of modern technology are a bit costly, especially compared to the $.49 cent stems they replace. At close to $125 a whack and you need five of them with a full-size spare, that adds a bit to the bottom line when you buy the car, and a lot to your tire bill when you replace them. They are also rather fragile, and if you put anything on them to cover them up, it must be made of plastic - metal covers apparently react with the metal in the stem and corrode them away in rapid fashion, causing them to leak and need replacement. I found this out the hard way and had to replace all four at a cost of nearly $600, something I'll not repeat for quite a while with any luck.

Thanks to these sensors, I noticed that one of the tires was losing air consistently, so since I just had the stems replaced, I took it back to where the work was done, thinking one of them might have been defective. I walk in the door to a Mr. Tire location near my house, tell them my saga, and they promise to take a look at it, but that there were a couple of people ahead of me - indeed for mid-week in late August, the waiting room was remarkably full, and some folks looked like they'd dug in for the long haul.

I waited only 45 minutes before I saw the car come around the front and a ticket with my keys and lug lock land on the front desk. I didn't even finish watching the day's episode of "The View" before they were writing me up - they had rebuilt the pesky little sensor valve, replacing a seal and the core, and remounting the valve, replaced the tire and buttoned it all up. They had under promised the waiting time by being vague, and had over-delivered by not just replacing the expensive part but by saving me lots of money by rebuilding the existing one.

What do my tires have to do with marketing? I'm now an evangelist, an auxiliary marketer for Mr. Tire - I'll recommend them to friends, I'll tell people about my experience (blog about it), use it as a landmark when giving directions, etc. Think what would happen to your business if all of your customers behaved this way about your product or service. The growth rate would be incalculable, your popularity unchallenged, your brand ubiquitous, your pockets forever full.

If you're a marketer, get out from behind your desk right now, take a stroll down to the customer service department and say a hearty "Thank You" to the folks that REALLY provide your reputation for you to customers. They are the real heroes, who do the job every day and don't get to have the creative fun that you do. They deserve a tip of your cap!

Good Customer Service Requires More Than Policy

I've often posited the theory that good customer service is the marketing department's greatest weapon. I also hold that the corollary opposite is true, that poor customer service can so turn off a customer, they boycott and spread the word to avoid the offending business. I recently got a taste of how this can work.

I needed a few bucks over the holiday weekend, and waited until I was on my way out on Monday to stop by a local bank and use their ATM machine. The machine not only refused to give me any cash or even register the transaction, but it kept my card, meaning I couldn't get cash anywhere else either. Not the greatest experience, but not a deal breaker, I could get by with what I had in my pocket for the day.

The bad part came the next morning, when I returned to the branch and asked for the card to be returned. I explained what had happened, and the branch staff informed me that while the gentleman responsible for emptying the machine wasn't due in until after lunch, they could not give me back my card, as it was a "foreign" card from another bank, and that it was "Bank Policy" to destroy those off brand cards once they had been withheld.

Three things wrong with this right off the bat.

1) ATM machines are fully networked, it doesn't matter what bank issued them as long as they are members of the same clearinghouse network; they should be fully recognized. This bank's machines had no difficulty taking my off-brand card on previous occasions and charged me a hefty fee for the privilege. Can't be that big a crime if they've accepted it in the past.

2) To hold and destroy a customer's property, especially something that by their own admission wasn't theirs, is particularly heinous, especially when there is no signage or verbiage informing ATM users of this practice.

3) To offer "It's Policy" as an explanation for such behavior, without further explanation, is the epitome of poor service. It smacks of powerless, cement-head, bureaucratic, paper-shuffling unresponsiveness that puts my hackles up and frustrates customers to no end. Not acceptable, under any circumstances.

I proceeded to the issuing bank and got the card replaced - in 7-10 days. Good thing it wasn't an emergency . . .!

The staff couldn't or wouldn't show me any such policy in any manual, wouldn't give me the name of anyone to contact about it, offered nothing but a stiff, insincere apology. Useless.

Now comes the marketing part - I know people who seek my advice or counsel on a variety of subjects, financial planning and money management among them. Rest assured that each time someone asks about how my bank is, do I like them, etc., I'll go out of my way to make sure that they avoid PNC, and that they tell all their friends to do the same. Unless they contact me directly (I wrote in to their automated customer service contact form, explaining the situation) and make me a convert, that practice will continue for the foreseeable future.

Just like the shampoo commercial says, you'll tell two friends, and they'll tell two friends, and so on, and so on . . . after a while their Hometown Bank will have to find a new home.

Suffice to say that be careful how you treat customers, they represent more than their own value as a customer.

Covering Your A** Leads to Lousy Customer Service

PNC bank actually followed up on my complaint outlined above. To wit:

"As this policy is not part of customer account disclosure, because it applies to both customers and non-customers, and is our internal security procedure, we are unable to provide a copy to you. Cards can be retained due to being reported lost or stolen, incorrect PIN attempts or being blocked by the bank of issue. PNC Bank would not be able to verify the reason for retention for a card issued by another institution. To avoid returning a stolen or blocked card, cards issued by any financial institution other than PNC Bank cannot be returned. This practice is employed by many other financial institutions as well."

All they had to do was ask me for my driver's license, or call Wachovia (the issuing bank) with me standing there and they could have avoided the whole mess. Such blanket policies rarely serve the customer, and are put in place to protect the bank. This way, no one has to think or make a judgment based on circumstances, they just say "it's policy" and they're off the hook. On the off chance that the card which still resided in their machine wasn't mine, there would really be no gain for the thief to return to the scene of the crime to retrieve a stolen card, as he couldn't use it the first time, and still couldn't use it now.

The big takeaway here is that to prevent the bad guys from doing something convoluted, they inconvenience the 99.9% of the rest of us who are honest, and make it policy to do so. Policies do not good customer service make - the most proficient businesses with the gold standard customer service empower their employees to solve problems based on case-specific information and to make judgment calls to help a customer. Good model to follow.

Are you listening, PNC?

Negotiation - the Spirit of Give and Take

Everyone negotiates, almost every day, on some level, even with themselves in some cases. The idea is to weigh two opposing ideas against each other and give up something one side needs to get something they want from them - simple, right?

Lawsuits are negotiations, divorce settlements, business contracts, even social gatherings (ever try to decide on a restaurant with a group of six people?). Everyday situations require at least some skill at negotiation, and really that's a good thing. It forces you to define your position on a given situation, to clarify your personal dividing line between "need" and "want," and forces you to devise rationale to defend your choices. Is it any wonder that decisive people are often the best negotiators?

One helpful hint in successful negotiation is to remove any emotion from the equation. This is difficult to completely accomplish, but the better you are at it, the more likely you are to get what you want. Emotion tends to cloud judgment, makes us do things for reasons other than logic or material gain, and to give in out of pity or caring for the others' well-being, even at risk to our own.

That doesn't mean that you can't be nice about it - nice isn't an emotion, it's a social convention. You can be civil and still not back off of your position and get what you want without emotionally wounding the other party. No need to be mean, just be firm and accommodating and civil, but stand your ground.

Above all, to be a negotiation, there has to be a spirit of give and take on both sides, some accommodation to the other side's position, some give in order to get. Without that willingness to cooperate, to lead the proceedings down a path to mutual agreement, then it's not a negotiation, it's an ultimatum. A this-is-it, take-it-or-leave-it approach will not produce the results either side wants. It engenders ill will between the parties and creates a very adversarial atmosphere that is counterproductive.

Sometimes, the situation just isn't conducive to negotiation. When one side holds all the power, all the cards, leaving the other side no real room to get and has little to give, negotiations will be strained and of limited value. Job interviews or evaluations for a pay increase are like this - the employee has little leverage in most cases, unless they are absolutely irreplaceable. The best they can hope for is to make a good case, show their value in a persuasive way, and hope the boss is feeling generous or sees potential in keeping the employee happy and productive. The one time where the employee has the whip hand in this relationship is during the initial salary negotiation after the offer is made. Market forces create variance in how much power the employer has, but the odds are always in their favor.

Successful negotiation requires knowledge - knowledge of self, knowledge of the opposition's position and wants, needs and desires. The better you know your own position, the more strongly you can negotiate it, because you have the surety of knowing where you draw the line, you have a picture of what you can live with, and anything above that is a bonus. If the other side's line is somewhere near yours, everybody wins at the end. A smart man once said "If both sides feel like they lost a little bit, it's a good deal" remarking to the spirit of willingness to give up something to get something else.

As you go through your week, take special note of situations that require you to negotiate - you might be surprised how many of them there are - and try to gauge how you might have used knowledge to improve your own position and get a better outcome . . . .

Want To Boost Profits? Never Mind Customer Satisfaction, Watch Your Rank

According to a study released by researchers at Fordham University and Ipsos Loyalty, customer satisfaction is not the best indicator of brand performance for consumer product or service companies. According to the study of 17,000 consumers over two years, the researchers developed a new measuring tool for brand effectiveness, dubbed the Wallet Allocation Rule, and skillful use of the principal can net companies millions of dollars, putting them ahead of their competitors and boosting recognition and loyalty along with customer engagement.

Apparently "satisfied" customers are not necessarily the most loyal or profitable. Wal-Mart found this out the hard way. After launching a major renovation initiative after reviewing massive amounts of customer feedback, it cleared aisles, deleted end caps, removed pallets of products and such, and sure enough, customer satisfaction scores rose - and same-store sales revenue entered the longest decline in store history! Apparently customers were happy to shop at Wal-Mart, but did a larger proportion of their shopping elsewhere. Share of "wallet" dissipated.

So if happy customers aren't loyal, and their happiness doesn't lead to spending, what does? Ranking of priority does, based on a simple formula that illustrates a high correlation between brand ranking and share of wallet, in a very predictable fashion. This takes into account not only the rank, where the consumer places your brand on the priority list, first, second etc., but also how many brands that do the same thing exist in the landscape of their shopping experience.

There is an elegant formula for calculating your rank, and for calculating your share of wallet, which I won't go into here. For details, see http://hbr.org/2011/10/customer-loyalty-isnt-enough-grow-your-share-of-wallet/ar/1 .

While the article states essentially that companies that boost their ranking will be more successful, what the formula doesn't tell you is how to boost the ranking of your brand upward. Based on the way they conducted the study, and our own research on the way consumers feel about brands, I can make some educated guesses. Consumers have an emotional connection to the brands they engage with, no matter how infrequently they cross paths. Most people won't admit to that connection or characterize it as emotional, but in interview research on brand awareness and delivery on the brand promise, consistently the brands with the highest emotional engagement, or most noticeable and consistent delivery on the promise would be the most popular, regardless of the nature of that emotion. Sometimes getting people riled up about something cements that brand sufficiently in consumers' minds to rank highly, due to the high level of emotional engagement, even though the emotion might appear negative.

The other factor at work here has more to do with awareness and visibility. The higher the frequency of engagement with a given brand, at least in brands that elicit a high emotional response, the higher the rank will be. Recency plays a part here, too, although not as big a part as you might think. If you've engaged with a brand more recently than others, that brand's ranking will tend to be higher, but only by a small percentage, and any negative aspect to the engagement will erode the recency effect almost immediately. That paradigm puts a lot of the responsibility for boosting brand ranking squarely in the Marketing Department. Marketing has long been the home of the brand steward, but this study gives some teeth to their feeling that "the more we spend the more we make". Big, vibrant, effective marketing campaigns that put product in consumer's hands more frequently and regularly, as long as the experience is living up to the promise, will move more units by boosting ranking, taking money away from your competitors and spiking share of wallet.

While consumer product or service sales is not a zero-sum game, you can grab market share from your competitors, and if you grab share of wallet, revenue and profits rise noticeably. Those extra sales had to come from somewhere, unless you're the only product in the category. Moral of the story is that you don't have to be the fastest guy in the jungle, you just have to be faster than the guy next to you, to avoid being eaten.

Chapter Takeaways:

1. Customer service is absolutely critical to the success of nearly every business, but especially those who sell directly to consumers on any level. It requires training and an investment in time and resources to treat customers with respect and compassion. Empowering customer service reps to actually solve customer problems and respond to complaints without permission or supervision is an imperative first step.

2. Just because you have a policy that covers a particular customer complaint, that doesn't mean that you can simply recite it and consider the customer 'served.' Policy is for guiding behavior and for training new employees. To really serve customers, the people responsible for interfacing with customers directly must have the responsibility, the duty and the authority plainly conferred to them, it must be theirs to own and use.

3. Customer service is a cultural phenomenon, and therefore starts at the top of the organization. To really be effective, it must be ingrained to the level that it's propensity is screened for at the hiring point and infuses every action each employee takes every day. It can be trained, but it is best showcased as a deeply ingrained personality trait that is expressed organically and naturally.

6) Direct Mail

Old Format Rises to the Occasion

I recently received a living anachronism in my mailbox - a local vendor card deck.

This format used to be much more popular, and was often used for Business-to-Business (B-to-B) lead generation 20-40 years ago. If you're younger and aren't familiar with these, they are a package of roughly 3"x5" lightweight cards, printed front and back, packaged up in shrink wrap like a candy bar, with one card acting as the "host" or sponsor and carrying the address block. Each card is a two-sided ad for a different local business, often themed around a group of industries or services pitched to a specific target group. For instance, if I were a deck publisher, and I was creating a deck to send to a list of recently changed addresses, I would likely target new movers by including paid ad cards from a roofer, a cleaning service, a painting company, a landscaper, paving contractor, pool company, lawn service, gutter sales and cleaning, chimney sweeps and other services that people moving into a new home or a new neighborhood might need.

This one appeared to be pitched not to new movers, but homeowners in general, as it is addressed to me or "Current Occupant" and contained cards from a fence contractor, a counter top company, a landscaper, a pool company, and several others surrounding home ownership and renovation.

I picked out maybe three vendors who were relevant to my life and my needs, and pitched the rest. The Host card offered a packaged up bundle of prizes by combining offers from three of the vendors, including a restaurant, a pool builder and an interior design firm. The offer isn't very explicit, but the slug line offers FREE dinner for two, and drives you to a website that will inevitably explain how these three go together to help me win a free dinner for two at the restaurant.

This format has lost popularity over the years, but at one time was quite lucrative. I know of direct mail publishers who churned out an industry-specific B-to-B deck every quarter, and went on vacation for two months until the next one needed to be put together. Once the ads are sold on a long-term one- or two-year contract, it's just assemble, print, package, mail. Pretty simple, but the list maintenance was pretty high, to keep response levels up and advertisers happy and coming back, and the level of detail to get a larger deck produced correctly is pretty high - it's like printing a magazine with no editorial and no binding.

With the advent of local look-up directories on the Internet, such decks as the one in my hand are anachronistic at best, but they must pull and make economic sense to the advertiser, or they wouldn't exist. Kudos to the publisher for making the math work for them and for keeping this format alive.

3D In Your Mailbox? Hollywood's a Bit Late To the Party!

Much of my practice involves implementing the strategies Granite Partners recommend to clients based on the research we perform for them, aimed at solving a specific problem or challenge they face. Many of these implementations have a direct marketing component to them, along with other media, for a full 360 degree integrated approach that reaches the target customer holistically from a number of different directions.

One of those directions, especially when working with a tightly defined target, a small in-house list of high-dollar purchasers, is dimensional mail. These little gems were the first 3D marketing in history and have been used for many decades to reach decision-makers. From pop-up books, to custom-crafted boxes and multi-panel packaging, these high-impact items deliver the message and cut through the clutter like nothing else.

We've recommended dimensional mail to clients who were seeking top management attention, selling to the C-suite, and trying to break through the maze, bust past gatekeepers, and escape the mail room, because they WORK!

The U.S. Post Office devoted almost an entire issue of "Deliver" magazine one month to these little beauties, and each case study includes the phrase something like "response rates were 300% of expected" or "we got more calls than we ever imagined" or "the extra up-front cost was no longer an issue based on the resulting sales". Can those phrases be applied to *your* last direct mail effort?

Creating dimension mail forces you to - dare I say it - think outside the box! Not only to you have all the usual guidelines for direct mail creative - stay on message, craft a clean offer, create interest and intrigue and urgency - but now you've got to think in three dimensions, think in layers of discovery by the recipient, think about production mechanics and weight and physics limitations, and a whole host of considerations, and still have it be effective, clever, creative and most of all profitable! It can be a head-scratcher, and a headache, but it's almost invariably worth the effort.

If you would like to explore how these creative solutions can boost sales or recognition for your firm, but don't have the background to do it yourself, call on someone like a consultant, to help you walk around the sink-holes and avoid the pitfalls, and let your creativity shine!

Hollywood's a little late to the 3D party, Direct Mail's been doing 3D for years!

Vacation Season is Selling Season

It's mid-August, and it seems like everything is slowing down a notch or two. A lot of people choose now for their summer vacations, while their children are out of school for a little longer, and the weather is good throughout most of the country. That means businesses are often seen as slower as well - with staff away from the office, calls don't get returned as readily, decisions are deferred and meetings planned for later in the year.

Now is the time to get to know your customers better, to set the stage for fourth-quarter year-ending activity. If your main contacts are in the office, now is the time to take them to lunch, hear about their plans for the fall and for next year, assure your place in the budgeting process, etc. Many non-profits are on a fiscal year basis lots of which end in October. That means budget time is now, so they have time to complete action planning, get approvals and get vendors proposals in place so they can plan their year.

If your main outreach is direct mail, typically the wisdom has been not to mail in August, and often that still holds - unless you're selling things to those going back to school, or travel supplies, or fall items like covers, wood racks, gardening supplies etc. Those folks are likely planning their next mailing and getting the elements together now to be ready to drop just a week before Labor Day. Delivery times are often longer due to reduced staffing in many parts of the country, especially for what used to be 3rd class mail, catalogs and such. Fortunately, delivery times for fulfillment items that are ordered have short-ened, so they can order from you and receive it in time to take the item to the beach for the long weekend! Dropping a little early doesn't hurt if you adjust your read time out accordingly. Many mailers see a delayed response to late summer mailings, but often a better one when all's said and done - just because they didn't read it when it arrived and they weren't home, doesn't mean they won't read it and respond later, when they're in a receptive mood after a nice trip to the shore or mountains and are recharged and ready to gear up for fall.

Other media, like TV and radio often experience some slack time this time of year, and there are some great bargains out there, largely a legacy from the old network seasonal model - Summer is for reruns and replacement shows. Cable line-ups have changed that model and you can still reach your target audience while watching new episodes of some of their favorites on A&E, Bravo, History or the Discovery channel. Radio, too has some great buys right now, as vacationing workers escape their morning commutes - but with driving vacations on the rise thanks to paid carry-ons, long security lines, and other airline shenanigans, you can still reach those folks in their cars, often with both decision-makers present, via radio. And, with national satellite networks in place and firmly established, you can get them wherever they're driving to, coast to coast.

Print stands a chance now too, as folks who've elected to stay home now have time to do a leisurely perusal of the morning paper or pick up those new issues of a magazine they've been neglecting. Maybe not quite as many sets of eyes, but often the right ones in a receptive mind frame is more productive.

Try new approaches, reconnect with customers, reach them in a new way, think up a new angle for an old product - Summer's here, and the time is right for marketing creativity! Time to toss out the rule book and make it shine!

Personalization Boosts Response, But Can Be Overdone

We've seen studies, a few released very recently, that suggest that personalization of direct marketing materials, including print and e-mail, boosts response significantly - in some cases as much as 3-400% of the blind "A" side of the test. But there was an interesting study among them that perhaps showed the risky downside to this type of approach. Apparently, personalization CAN be overdone. But you'd be surprised how far you have to go . . . !

The study we read told of a direct marketing control package that had been declining from fatigue after nearly six months of heavy mailing. The commissioners of the test decided to test personalization, but in a new way. They personalized the letter in multiple places, and progressively added incidents of personalization as the letter progressed, per segment of the test. Segment One was mailed to a random list select of the house list, and contained a personalized greeting. Segment Two was mailed to a similar random list pull but the letter had a greeting and another incident further into the body of the letter that was personalized. Segment Three was mailed to a similar list and contained three incidents of personalization, and so on. All data was composed of elements contained in the address block of a five-line address containing job title and company name.

When the results were read and analyzed, the staff was astonished to see response rates continue to rise through segment 14! In a two-page marketing letter there were fourteen instances of personalization before the results started to flag. The package didn't drop back below profitability until Segment 22! Clearly, people like reading about themselves, and as a result, feel you know them and are safe to buy from! The rise of the rate was roughly linear from one incident to 14, and tailed off sharply from 14 to 22 and dropped off less sharply after that. Seems it takes a lot to overdo personalization, at least as used in this study.

I get the feeling that most mail package probably wouldn't get to 14 before dropping off, based on how much imagination is usually put behind this portion of the marketing effort. Just dropping the name in the copy 14 times is not going to do it! To test this, simply read the letter out loud to yourself. Have you ever been engaged with a retail sales person who had only gotten partially through their "Training" but got to the part where they were told to use the customer's name whenever possible to help "connect" with the customer on a personal level? The overuse of your name in the conversation in unnatural places becomes annoying, then grating, then off-putting to the point where you want to stop the interaction and walk away.

With that experience in mind, read your letter out loud and see at what point your tolerance for the use of your name and other info seems to peak. Now, subtract one incidence, and that's likely the sweet spot for that particular letter or package. Now you have a baseline, and can test above and below that number and see how accurate your initial read was.

Keep in mind, too that there is a gold mine of information in that address block, if you're willing to make a few leaps. If you have accurate salutation and prefix information, you likely know marital status, gender, and to some extent, age. Ms. Brittany Jacobs isn't likely to be 75, or married, or likely to buy orthopedic shoe inserts or support hose. You get some of this at least in a reinforcing capacity, from your list segmentation selections. And you can use all parts of the address block beyond the address. There are data overlays that can be appended based on zip code that can give you a read on income, age, and other data down to the block level. Combine that with the job title info, and you have a pretty good picture of your prospect. Use street names, city and state info, job title, whatever you can to build a box of credibility around your offer. Now you just have to find a creative way to work those elements into the conversation so that they appear to be accurate but are really vague. If you're having trouble with this, try imagining you're setting up a fortune teller booth at a carnival - they use this same technique to read cues from you to weave a story that sounds believable. It's like they KNOW you!

This may seem deceptive, or underhanded, sneaky, etc. but ethically all you're doing is making some educated guesses, and feeding the information you have that is freely available back to the audience on a specific basis - nothing sneaky about that! Let your creativity run wild, build a conversation with as much credible personalization as you can - you'll find it gets harder once you get above 7-8 incidents. And now that you know that the average person's tolerance level is higher than that, go for it!

Test personalization on your next package, and see how much it boosts your response - in today's digital world, there's no reason not to . . .

Integration and Personalization Keys to Success

Every marketer is trained from the beginning of his/her career to attempt to get the most value from their marketing dollars - everyone knows that dollars are scarce enough without wasting them! Usually that means running leaner, tightening expenses, negotiating fees, cutting costs, avoiding waste. These measures assume that there is nothing you aren't doing to boost performance, increase awareness or response, extend reach or build frequency, expose the brand more widely or selectively. One of the most effective strategies we've seen pay off is media integration to drive support of the central message.

As it turns out, American audiences like a choice. Who knew . . .? But good direct marketers know that if you offer a prospect too many choices, they may make none at all. No joy there. But if you offer them a choice and they don't know you've done it, everybody wins. That's what media integration is all about, creating those choices in the background. And, as an added bonus, which choice the buyer makes tells you something about them, absolutely FREE!

Picture a barstool (don't lie, we *KNOW* you've seen them). They have three or four legs and a seat, or platform. The level of effectiveness of that device degrades in direct proportion to the number of legs - start removing legs and the stool gets less stable to the point where it won't stand alone, or even becomes dangerous. You *can* sit on a one-legged stool, but it's not for the faint of heart! On the other hand, a five or six-legged stool can become unwieldy or unstable too - keeping all those legs the same length and flat is a challenge, or at best the extras are redundant and wasteful.

What do barstools have to do with marketing? An integrated campaign to build awareness or drive enrollment or response can have several types of media integrated, each adding to the stability, and the effectiveness of the campaign, each message supporting the other media and the offer platform, like the legs of the stool.

Say you were promoting a conference. You have a great list of prospective attendees, responsive, accepting of the brand, happy evangelists for your organization. You have good, extensive file info in each record, including phone number, mailing address, e-mail address, some transactional info and more.

You've got a terrific speaker line-up, a highly relevant topic, a great location. Sounds like you've got a good shot at success, but here's how to maximize the number of bodies in those seminar seats - tell the prospect about the conference in multiple ways using different media.

You could mail to them, and the mailing could include a Personalized Uniform Resource Locator (PURL) that leads to a personalized landing page that showed their participation with your organization in the past year (or what they missed, in the case of a newbie). You could also send them a personalized e-mail with a slightly different PURL link embedded in it, one that drives them to another page that shows their best choice in hotels or dinner location. You could also launch a robo-call or volunteer phone bank call a few days before the conference, directing them to the registration site for a last minute discount on airfare from a consolidator/partner. The e-mail also has a phone number included for audio registration, the e-mail has a reply feature for questions, the phone call lists an e-mail address as well as the web registration site address, and the registration page has a phone number for inquiries. You've now come at the prospect from three different directions, sent essentially the same message (attend this great conference) but shown them different facets of the conference, shown the benefits in the outgoing vehicles, and given them a choice as to how to respond to you (mail, reply e-mail, web registration, return phone call). Plus, the way they choose to respond or register tells you what mode of communication is the most convenient or effective for them, information you can use to reach them more effectively next time - FREE!

Those three directions are the legs of the stool - each media supports the message platform, and feeds the other media: web, e-mail, voice, print mail. This sort of campaign might make it tougher to discern just exactly what is driving response, but as long as the response is strong and the meeting is full, the job is done, and most of these are trackable now so that dilemma isn't as problematic as it once was.

You can drive response to one media or another, but giving the prospective attendee a choice as to how they want to respond increases your odds of a response almost exponentially. Personalizing each medium makes each more effective than the generic version, further strengthening the campaign. By adding to your integration scheme with low-cost supports, (e-mail, and volunteer phone calls) you've maximized your resources and gotten the most bang for your buck, in some cases doubling or tripling your effectiveness, without doubling the cost.

Check the campaigns you have running and see if they could benefit from an integrated approach. It may be a little more work, even if you re-purpose elements like graphics, copy, forms, e-mail templates etc. but the results are definitely worth it.

Get Top Results When You Crank Up the "Direct" in Your Direct Mail

By its very nature, direct mail promotions are designed to be one-to-one communication vehicles. As marketers, we are all aware of this in the back of our minds, but in practice, sometimes the "direct" portion drops off the map, and we end up producing unplaced promotional brand ads in an envelope. If you want o see the best returns possible from your direct mail program, make sure the "Direct" angle gets full attention.

There are several ways to rev up the "you" in your programs. The most effective one starts with the concept of the mailing itself. As you envision the final mailing, conceptualize your offer, the list, the copy platform, the thematic graphics and other elements, get a good fix on your target audience for this particular mailing.

The "It" Person

Now take this to the next level, and picture in your mind a specific individual who fits the descriptors and parameters of your typical customer in your target market. Ask some key questions about your mailing with regard to this person: 1) Would this mailing appeal to this person? 2) Is the offer suitable for them and their needs? 3) Would this copy and these graphics attract their attention and resonate with them in an emotional way? 4) Is there enough reason for them to respond, to pay, to write a check and send it in?

If the answer to any of those questions is no for that mythical person in your head, then adjust, correct, edit and revamp until the answer is yes to all of them.

Copy is King

Many of these personal elements start with the copy. Often, the offer is what it is, and either can only be changed minimally to match the audience or is inviolate based on the time and resources available. If you're in that box, then the solution is to start with the copy.

The word "You" is extremely powerful - indeed, you can't write a true direct mail piece without it. If your copy speaks directly to that person in your mind, you are by fiat having that one-to-one conversation, and must use "You" to address that person directly, in first person voice. In today's highly digital climate, the use of a person's name in the copy is almost passé, but you would be surprised how little it actually gets used, aside from personalized laser letters. For postcards, fixed multipage packages, and other formats, digital technology allows for the use of the recipient's name and other information in repeated appropriate fashion, to juice up your message and really push the audience's emotional buttons. This will drive your point home almost as powerfully as the word FREE in the offer, and will draw in the reader and involve them in your description and your message.

Good copy for direct mail should tell a story. Listing benefits, describing features has its place, but the meat of the piece is a message directly specifically at the reader like there is no one else around, and it's just the two of you having a short conversation. The story should be illustrative, persuasive, cohesive, and have a point. No matter how long it is, (and there are endless debates about copy length – see Hershel Gordon Lewis for details on both sides) you should make a point, explain why your point is the best, make your point again, and get out after asking for the order.

Let the Data Be Your Guide

To be able to write persuasive, effective copy, to concoct an effective working offer, you have to really know the audience. You can get to know the audience, but to do that, some research is in order. Carefully select your list to be as homogeneous as possible, to select as many similarities as you can to define the audience as finely as you can. That list of selects is the basis for your research. In order to get to know those people (and a market never bought anything, people buy products), you have to have an actual conversation with a few of them, to pick up the subtleties, the similarities and the things that really push their buttons emotionally that get them going, that get them excited.

To help visualize the audience better, pretend to have a conversation with ,someone representative of the target group, and ask yourself these questions:

1) How does this person speak, what word choices do they make?

2) How do they synthesize the information you are presenting? Do they parrot it back to you verbatim, or do they absorb, summarize and paraphrase your concepts?

3) Do they pick up and use any jargon you use related to the product?

4) Does the product seem to be something they need, or just want?

5) Do they seem to understand the product you are offering or are they just being polite?

These ideas should give you plenty of ammunition with which to shoot down your current work and start from scratch, to really personalize your direct mail and make them truly "Direct" to the audience. Apply these techniques to your last project, recreate it with the new approach, and A/B test it against your control – you will be surprised at the results.

Chapter Takeaways:

1. Direct mail is a time-honored marketing activity that has seen its popularity wax and wane over the years, but that remains a viable way to reach out to customers and convert prospects.

2. Careful practice of direct mail marketing requires that the effort be viewed as a one-to-one communication between the company and the recipient – it's *direct* mail, and the more direct you can make the communication, the more likely it is to resonate with the consumer and to activate a purchase.

3. Testing is the bedrock upon which a good direct mail program is built. Test every aspect of the program, from lists, to copy, to graphics, to delivery dates, to number and type of inserts, to offers and premiums. The more you test, the more you know, and the less expense you have to mail, and the more profitable the mailing program will be.

7) Media/Advertising

Publish or Perish - By What Definition?

In today's social media-immersed, blogosphere saturated, media-driven, net savvy world, the nature of publishing has certainly changed. The very definition of publishing has changed as well - but is that a good thing?

The Internet has provided the everyman a unique opportunity to broadcast his/her innermost thoughts to the world, no matter how inane or irrelevant, with no editing, correction or restraint. While this may seem freeing, in the end it has lead to a huge, nearly unnavigable mass of questionably valuable information. Now when researching a topic, you certainly have more information available and in a more convenient format - but is it valid, accurate, vetted, and unbiased? Probably none of the above in most cases.

This glut of information has given rise to some unique phenomenon as well - the speed with which urban legends develop and spread is breathtaking compared to just a decade ago. Viral information can be more damaging than real viruses, and travels faster, and with greater impact! Cyber-bullying is now an additional concern parents have to deal with, and the youth of today have diluted the accuracy, eloquence and power of their native English nearly to the point of unintelligibility, in the interest of speed and convenience, holding true to an artificially-imposed brevity limit. Progress . . .?

Internet publishing has some tremendous advantages, in speeding the exchange and sharing of scientific, philosophical, cultural, economic, and ideological information. In the old days, when a book or magazine article was "published" in print, a whole host of scholarly, educated, experienced professionals read, fact-checked, edited, contributed to and proofed a work before it was released to the public. This may have slowed the release of information, but it gave the information a fighting chance to be at least passably accurate and honest. Today, most of those professionals have been rendered obsolete, and those skills are rolled up into a single individual - the author, right or wrong.

What does all this have to do with marketing? Simply this: take care in assessing what you "put out there" to market your company, build your brand, promote your products - one false step not only travels faster than you can catch, but is permanent, residing in servers and living on hard drives around the world!

Internet Not the Only Media - Yet

In a recent study of college freshmen, it was revealed that the skills we once assumed to be vital for business success - research using books and journals, proper grammar when writing letters, crafting informational documents or publishing and the like - are now obsolete, and that over 90% of college freshmen don't possess them. They also noted that e-mail communication is already deemed "too slow" by today's college freshmen, who have no concept of television with less than 250 channels, having been born in 1992, long after the cable expansion and the introduction of satellite TV.

These same freshmen have never possessed a record album, or conceivably a pre-recorded music CD, having come into their teens after the original MP3 file format was introduced. Fax machines are obsolete antiques, land-line phones passé, and with them phone etiquette similarly out the window. Pay phones are a mystery, a story told around campfires . . . you get the picture. Technology, especially in the communication world, has accelerated at a remarkable rate, leaving behind what seemed to be perfectly viable formats and forms of communication.

These same college freshmen, who don't know from cassettes, will be entering the workforce in four short years, and a small percentage of them potentially taking on tomorrow's marketing challenges. By that time, full media integration that has been trumpeted as the be all and end all of communication technology may be in place on a national or global scale, and there will essentially be one, web-driven media, all played wirelessly through whatever monitoring device happens to be handy, be it a plasma TV, the screen in the car, or the front of the refrigerator. Everything will have an IP address, from the phone to the washing machine. Everyone will have to be a web producer, a video producer, or designer, and every speech or form of communication will be measured in megabytes or terabytes, not in pages or words.

Grammar is already slipping at an alarming rate, with proper forms of English dropping off the cultural map like electronic flies, to be replaced by slang, initials, acronyms and emoticons - we're slowly sliding back to early Egyptian hieroglyphs. How do you diagram the phrase "LOL :)!" ?

The ads of the future will only have to be produced for electronic consumption, and will be a mix of images and scrolling, hopping, swinging and fading text, compressed down to the smallest file size possible and distributed through three big outlets. Print will be an anachronism, copywriting a dead art, direct mail reserved for senior citizen newsletters and billing inserts in large print, with ads flashing on big, wall sized screens in all the retirement homes, which will automatically change to match the information emanating from a chip in their forearm as the seniors walk by, ala Minority Report. Well, maybe not that last one in four years, but you get the idea.

With only one medium to consider, media buying will consolidate into a government function controlled by the FCC, and time will be bid on in auction style on E-Bay. Marketers will no longer have to consider paper stock weight, envelope size, postal rate case, number of sheets on a billboard, magazine doubletruck gutters, facing page competitors, color fidelity, dot gain, screen density, and a host of other routine, mundane production detail-oriented skills required by the marketers of yesteryear. Freed from those details, will the ads be more persuasive, more effective, more targeted, more efficient? They will certainly be trackable, which is an advantage, but my guess is that how that tracking can be used will have to be heavily regulated to prevent rampant abuse.

I'm not much of a futurist, but I am a student of history, and you can easily compare the current communications integrity status to that of the latter stages of the Roman Empire - I'm breaking out my fiddle as we speak . . . !

Are You Prepared for a Communications Crisis?

In the general hierarchy of life's priorities when you think of crisis, the marketing department is probably not the place to call. But if you're a business that's facing a natural disaster, a tampering case involving your products, an on-the-job accident or other damaging event, that call to the marketing department is one of the first and most important. But if they aren't prepared to handle a communications crisis, it may not help.

Is your company prepared for a scramble drill in communicating effectively to convey the proper information, using the right tone and messaging to quell customer fears, or creditor agitation or anxiety, and deal with intrusive media inquiries? If not, now might be a good time to craft a plan, get it reviewed and vetted by all other departments for accuracy and feasibility and get it put in place - before the crisis occurs.

This plan should include the following:

1) **List of personnel involved:** Who is the designated spokesman for your company, who comes next if that person is not available? Create the hierarchy so that the job tumbles downhill logically. The person needs to be credible, well-spoken, and to understand the goals and ideals of the company thoroughly so that any statement made to the local or national media is believable and makes sense.

2) **Who internally should be contacted:** List of people will vary depending upon the nature of the crisis, but at bare minimum, the CEO, CFO, VP Operations, General Manager, VP Marketing, and in-house Counsel should be included on the list. Your plant security company should be informed immediately, and if the crisis involves injury or death of staff or contractors on the site, the local police department, local first responder services if needed, and local utilities that service the site, including Hazmat services if required.

3) **What is your position on the incident?** Is it an accident, was it intentional sabotage, is your company responsible in any way, what is your plan going forward? From a public relations standpoint, clarity and direct honesty is always the best policy. The media is tremendously resourceful, and they will find out

their version of the truth. Better to give them yours and it turns into a non-story, than to stonewall and let them start digging on their own.

4) **Provide only the facts you're sure of.** If you don't know for certain, simply tell the media that you're investigating and will keep them informed as things develop in that investigation. Make sure in-house counsel or your of-counsel attorney reviews any written statements for accuracy, or anything that legally obligate your company to do anything in future.

5) **Position Your Company As Compassionate, Caring, Concerned.** No matter how simple or harmless the situation appears, in today's environment anyone can potentially be construed as a victim of something. Make sure your company is seen as one that cares about all its employees and contractors, or any civilians who may have inadvertently been involved in the incident. Spread the net of concern wide, but make no direct promises, express your concern for the well-being of all, and stress that no matter the cause or level of responsibility your company ultimately takes in the final analysis, they will take great pains to assist and care for anyone affected by the incident.

The real trick is to have a speedy, comprehensive and clear position, and to release it to the media as early as possible. If media representatives sense that you're holding back or hiding something in any way, they will see it as their duty to get to "the truth" as they see it. Fast response heads this reaction off at the pass, returns control to your hands, and makes it appear that you know the drill and are being cooperative.

Each crisis is different, and each calls for a custom-tailored response. But if you have a plan of action, centralized contact information, a chain of command and a prepared spokesman, you can contain most incidents and concentrate on damage control to preserve your company's reputation and good name.

Fundamentals Can Save Your Advertising Program

As a consultant, I read – a lot – every day, about different marketing approaches, different angles and aspects of marketing, from social media trends to mobile, to automated e-mail, to article marketing, and a huge variety of other things that bombard my in-box every day, both electronically and in the snail mail and online. With all that reading and absorbing comes some inherent sense of how current corporate professionals in the marketing field are going about their work, what they focus on, what they feel is important, what's hot and what's out of fashion.

In all that absorption, I get to analyze how those marketers work, and how effective their efforts are. I also get called upon to critique their work from time to time, and let them know how a "knowledgeable" audience might view their performances. I was judging a series of ads the other day for a survey of magazine ads and their effectiveness, and I was amazed at how many of the Business-to-Business ads didn't incorporate even the most fundamental, basic elements that should be in *all* advertising. Top professionals at high-priced agencies were creating ads read by, and hopefully responded to, by other professionals – and there were lousy headlines that were far from compelling if there was one at all, lists of product features with no associated benefits, copy that was difficult to decipher, let alone read and be persuaded by, and a host of other ills that most freshman marketers have a good handle on by year two. I was amazed and astounded that large, profitable companies with marketing departments staffed with educated, qualified professionals were paying for this level of performance from their agencies, or worse, producing this kind of product themselves!

Sure, it's easy to rely on others to cover the basics, and you hope that the high-paid pros know better and they shouldn't need much supervision. And it's easier still to simply look at last year's or last week's effort and say, "yeah, good enough, run that one again" and perpetuate the poor construction, bad design, lousy and ineffective headlines, poorly-written copy that is neither persuasive or compelling. If it wasn't, we'd be out of business. But the truth is, if these pros had simply focused on the fundamentals, their work would improve in both effectiveness and creativity.

1) **Get me involved.** Write a real headline, one that compels me to read further, that poses a problem a challenge, asks a question, declares a position or benefit.

2) **Write and design it so even I can read it.** Real type fonts, in a decent size, in a contrasting color, either in columns, wrapped around an image, bannered at the top or bottom, somewhere that my eye can track and make sense of. Make it compelling, readable, persuasive, tell me how it will make my life easier, faster, better, lighten my workload, solve a problem, keep me sane, let me sleep at night, beef up my paycheck, cut my expenses. Tell me the benefits of the product or service, not just what it includes or is comprised of. Tell me something to make me feel I "need" what you're selling, hopefully leading me to . . . buy!

3) **Include a call to action I can respond to.** I get through the headline, it drives me to read the copy to learn more, it ends, and . . . nothing! Give me a phone number, a specific web address, an e-mail or physical address, an offer of some kind, a place to go to learn more, see the product, make a purchase, someone to call to order one, something!

4) **Lay it all out so it naturally drives me to that offer.** Americans read left to right, top to bottom, it's deeply ingrained in our psyche to do so, so that we may all absorb information in uniform fashion. Don't fix it if it isn't broken, start at the top, (it's called a headline for a reason) and work your way down. Leave the collages for grade school, keep the fancy special effects for the YouTube video - just design it in a way that is pleasing to the eye and supports the other elements.

5) **Make the images and the text support each other and work TOGETHER to get your point across.** I can't tell you how many ads I reviewed that contained an image that had virtually no bearing on what was being sold or discussed. It was either a product shot with no identification or name, no branding, or known function or relevance to the headline or offer, or a shot of some landscape or character that had no real bearing on what was being discussed. You've spent a lot of time and money finding, modifying or creating that image, make it work to your advantage to help sell the concept or idea you're conveying.

Just following these five guidelines will improve your publication and print advertising immeasurably, and put you ahead of 70% of the highly paid agency professionals that crank out B2B ads on their lunch hour . . . you might even make a sale!

Integration Is Key to Marketing Campaign Effectiveness

The phrase "The whole is greater than the sum of its parts" is never more appropriate than as part of a discussion of integrated marketing campaigns. No matter how you slice it, by media type, by audience, by offer type or any other way, multiple approaches working together with common offers, common brand and common goal will be much more effective than any of those single efforts, and even more than all of them working independently. At the risk of using an overused term, there is "synergy" to be gained by driving all efforts under the same flag.

Integration offers several key benefits, which as marketers we can scarcely afford to ignore.

1. **Cost-effectiveness**. If a greater return (be it registrations, hits, impressions, memberships, sales, etc.) is gained by fewer outgoing exposures (mail pieces, ads, radio spots, e-mails, phone calls) because they work together and support each other, then the same results have been obtained for less expense. More for less is the goal, and this hits it squarely.

2. **Breadth of Coverage**. If point one is true (and I stipulate that it is) then the corollary is that for the same cost, you can reach out to even broader audience. This spreads the brand and the offer further, which can be beneficial to the next effort beyond this initial one, preconditioning the new audience to respond the next time they are touched.

3. **Brand Strength.** Based on point two, if you are reaching more people with an integrated campaign, the pieces supporting each other, the brand impression is strengthened with each hit – overlap is more likely, and the impression is stronger with each hit as a result – there's no disconnect between impressions depending upon the piece to which the audience is exposed.

Some of the strength of campaign integration comes down to brand control. Harley Davidson has one of the strongest brands on earth, and its customers and fans are among the most loyal purchasers around. One reason for that effect is that the brand itself is so highly protected. All licensing is strictly enforced, and that HD moniker in all its various forms can ONLY appear on products that fit the brand profile. That kind of control creates a strong continuity. That brand on any product means that you can expect a certain level of quality, a certain outward attitude, a certain value and an appeal that competing products don't have. An integrated campaign uses that same power of continuity and of meeting expectation as part of its effectiveness.

Another big strength of integrating a campaign is to drive more response from the fringes of the target at no additional cost. If each segment of a campaign is independent, some slivers of the audience may slip through the resulting cracks in coverage between segments. If one medium fails to reach and motivate a member of the target population, if another does hit at a later time, the recognition level will be lower because the look, feel, fit, offer or appearance are not the same. No gain for that second piece. On the other hand if that first effort hits but fails to motivate, when the second, but integrated hit comes along, it has higher chance of being effective and motivating a usable response, because the recognition level is higher.

It's All About Levels

Integration can be achieved on a number of levels. Ideally, a tight effective campaign should be tied together on all of them to maximize return on investment.

Level 1 – Appearance

All pieces in all mediums (except radio) should have a similar look and feel to them, including type face, imagery, color palette, theme, copy voice, and should offer the same product at the same terms, should share contact information (same phone number, e-mail address, website address etc.) for response, and include the same expression of the product and company logotype. First glance continuity will go a long way toward boosting that recognition and beefing up response numbers.

Level 2 – Functionality

Each piece should not only function on its own to drive response, but cross-promotes to drive response from the other approaches as well. Fast food advertising is often good at this technique. You see the spot on television, which drives you to the website for more details, which drives you to the restaurant to use the coupon from the web, which is emailed after a registration process. These three media are functionally tied together in this campaign. The TV spot, the website, the e-mail and the point of purchase materials all have the same offer, the same appearance and you are engaged by all four to drive a purchase. The added bonus is that along the way you're also exposed to a full range of other related products, thus priming the pump for an extended purchasing relationship.

Level 3 – Emotionality

This is the toughest to achieve, but if the campaign is truly integrated it becomes extremely effective. Emotionality describes the emotion, the feeling elicited by the campaign. Each piece, each media contact, each touch-point with the customer should elicit that same emotional response. And at its peak, not only should the same emotion be activated, but the customer should feel it at the same level of intensity as the initial contact.

Say for example you receive a direct mail piece from a company selling fitness equipment. You're interested in losing weight and getting fit. The next day you see a TV spot for the same piece of equipment with even more information and a fuller set of benefits, shown to you in living color, and you're pumped up all over again. That afternoon on the radio driving to the grocery store you hear a radio spot for that equipment. When you get excited, and when you get to the organic foods aisle of the grocery, you see a dispenser with coupons for $10 off organic foods for owners of that equipment, just by sending in the coupon or going online and registering with your equipment's serial number. You've gotten that same level of excitement in all five cases, and it's driven you to seek out the equipment and make the change in your life, for purely emotional reasons – there are probably lots of different pieces of equipment that would provide the exercise you need, but that one got you excited in a repeated, intensive way at a very deep emotional level, and kept up that intensity throughout all the different media and offer sets. That's a truly effective integrated campaign, and it provides maximum return for your marketing dollar.

All three levels offer advantages over the traditional, less coordinated campaign. The higher a level of engagement you can achieve, the higher the level of effectiveness you're going to experience. There is a direct correlation between the degree of integration you can achieve compared to response levels among the target audience.

Level I offers significant gains over any single medium alone, and is the most cost effective, in terms of the number of different media used and the level of effort required compared to cost to execute.

Level II requires a bit more in terms of resources, but can provide a strong boost in response, especially for existing programs that have some brand awareness among the target audience but that need some refreshing to re-engage the audience.

Level III requires a very strong effort to coordinate all the various elements, to time them to launch together, and requires more media exposure initially to drive traffic toward the goal, but the ultimate response level can be incredibly high. Double-digit responses from the selected target are not unusual, and on higher-ticket offers that can represent significant revenue.

Of course, all of this coordination and integration cannot happen without the

technological infrastructure in place to support it. The databases involved in handing off the leads from one medium to another, the online backbone and processing software that allows prospects to see exactly what they are supposed to see when visiting the target site, to be able to take advantage of offers referred by other medium, to be able to print custom coupons with matching response codes and list numbers, and all the rest of the necessary back end that provides the intelligence for all the activity behind the scenes cannot be overlooked.

Overall, integration is a valuable key to attaining pushdown marketing response levels that are unrivaled by singular media levels. The extra expense and effort at the outset provides significant payback in the long-term, and sets the stage to expand your efforts to new products, new approaches and the creation of an extremely loyal purchasing audience for a long time to come.

Chapter Takeaways:

1. Digital media has taken a prominent place in the panoply of media choices advertisers have to choose from today. The meaning of the word publishing has changed in the last three decades, and its function as a communications vehicle has changed as well.

2. Public Relations programs can do more than just raise visibility for your company. An emergency communications plan is critical for the care and feeding of your brand, simplifying damage control in the event of an emergency and assuring that the proper response is issued and made public at the appropriate time.

3. Advertising is a time-honored method of corporate outreach and has developed into a near science, one that some agencies and businesses practice with great aplomb and some struggle with their entire lives. A return to the basics is always helpful, to refresh concepts and refocus on the core of the mission – to reach and persuade customers.

8) Tradeshows/Event Marketing

Event Marketing Takes a Step Forward

In the interest of full disclosure, I have to mention that I have a soft spot in my marketer's heart for event marketing endeavors - having grown one of the nation's largest industrial tradeshows into a top ten winner in five years, I know how hard it is to get "butts in the seats, bodies in the aisles" at a convention or tradeshow – especially when the audience has very little holding it together in terms of common interest except the desire to be more successful by learning from those who are already.

In my mailbox recently was a piece of direct mail that takes a format rarely seen used in event marketing – the laminate.

The piece is promoting the "Get Motivated" Business Seminar, coming in a week or so to 1st Mariner Arena, featuring an august line-up of speakers, including Rudy Giuliani, Sarah Palin(?), Steve Forbes, Tamara Lowe, Michael Phelps, Joe Gibbs, Zig Ziglar (R.I.P.) Michael Oher, and General Colin Powell. Wow, talk about your star-studded event!

The piece caught my eye not because of the speaker line-up, as there were full page ads running in business publications and the *Baltimore Sun* for the last two to three weeks promoting the event, but because of the format. The piece is about 11" x 6" in full color, promoting this series of motivational presentations on various topics, with die-cut portraits of each of the speakers, front and back, and is fully laminated with heavy plastic, also die-cut to the outline. This piece makes very efficient use of limited real estate, and includes two testimonials, a special offer box, the actual offer, a cash drawing giveaway, a mail panel, three movie-style reviews, and the phone number, web address, price, promo code and logistical information including dates , time, and location, all in that small space. Somebody thought this out extremely well, spent time and money to execute it, and took great care of those little details we mentioned yesterday.

Based on the speaker line-up, this can't be a one-off performance, it's gotta be a road show, so they must be replicating this in other cities and just changing the logistical info from place to place, to get the volume needed to make this cost-efficient to produce and mail. It takes quite a bit to get folks around here to give up an entire day at work, spend $5, go down to the Arena, park, and spend the day listening to motivational speakers.

Kudos to whoever put this together, this and the ads and other media are all well-executed and professional – I hope you filled the seats!

This is how event marketing should be done. It turns out that it takes about seven different exposures to move a prospect from idea to order when considering attending an event, business or otherwise. Public entertainment like the circus, Broadway shows, concerts, movies and other one-time events require at least that to get your attention. Business and industrial event marketers rarely spend the money or take the time in advance to create circumstances that bring their event in contact with the prospective audience seven times – it's very expensive, and time consuming, and you have to know all the information before you start - circumstances that rarely occur in non-profit and industrial event marketing. Speakers are added late, session descriptions don't arrive until late, schedules change, sponsors get added mid-way – about the only things you're sure of are the location and the dates, maybe the price. As more pieces are created, more information is included, evolving as they disseminate the information to the likely audience many times in relatively close proximity on the calendar.

Registrants are enrolling and buying tickets closer and closer to the actual event than ever before, thanks to online ticketing, will-call windows and credit card reservations, travel consolidators and last-minute deals on hotels and airfare. This makes it doubly frustrating for event marketers, as they get a delayed effect when measuring response to their efforts. You might not see a single ticket sale until the third marketing effort due to this effect. This makes it hard to test concepts, and even with promo codes and other devices, it's hard to tell what piece or vehicle is actually driving response. It relies on a cumulative effect of all the efforts to create a general widespread and trustworthy picture in the prospect's mind before they make a decision to buy a ticket. Tough sledding for marketers trying to full arenas and hotel ballrooms . . . .

Don't get me started on "destination" marketing! Just Don't - 'nuff said.

Event Marketing - The Key to Reaching New Customers May Be Through Their Stomachs

If you own or operate a service or manufacturing business, one great way to show your leadership of your industry and in the local business community is to host an event. There are many benefits, little downside, and, if successful, it can be scaled up or down or repeated again and again.

There are some basic requirements for a successful event:

1) **Guests!** Getting enough participation by the right participants is key. Market the event extensively, but create exclusivity by sending actual paper invitations - not just an e-mail announcement of an open house. The invitation requests and begs an RSVP, so that you can get an accurate head count for food and beverage, space planning etc. You want the room to look full but not crowded, and you'd like current customers to mix and mingle with prospects, so they spread the word about the work you do for them.

2) **Refreshments.** This is a tough part for many people to get right. Gauging the amount, level and type of food and drink to serve a very diverse guest list can be difficult, but there are some guidelines to follow to make it easier.

a) Let the time of day for the event guide your choices. For afternoon events, light appetizers and soft drinks may be appropriate. For an after-hours cocktail event, more substantial appetizers and passed hors d'oeuvres and beer and wine selections might be more appropriate.

b) For a dinner event or awards presentation, a buffet style will facilitate networking, but a sit-down dinner will allow guests to be more comfortable for a longer period of time, and form fewer but closer relationships with table-mates. Get the highest quality food and most sophisticated beverage choices you can afford - these are your guests and customers, doubly important to let them know you care enough to serve the best.

c) Drinks. For open bars, plan on two to three drinks per person, average, and keep key brands of each spirit on hand, along with plenty of mixers. For gatherings of over 20 people, hire a professional bar tender, you don't want your guests being over-served because your staff feels generous when pouring for their favorite customer. Keep plenty of ice on hand, about two pounds per person is a good rule of thumb.

3) **Venue.** If you are a manufacturing business, you have hard assets to show off – an open house type should include a "plant tour" of your production areas and equipment. Clean up extensively beforehand, remove trash, scrap and waste, remove any unused or non-functional equipment, sweep and mop floors, remove signage or decoration of questionable taste from walls, re-install any safety equipment, cover or hide proprietary customer work in progress. If you're a service business, there may not be much of interest to show visitors, cubicles look the same pretty much everywhere. Consider having the event in your building lobby if it is impressive, or at a nearby hotel.

4) **Entertainment.** Unless this is strictly an open house to greet customers, there should be some additional component to the event to warrant attendance by the guests. If you seek to be a thought leader in your industry or local business community, consider a brief presentation by your top management, including slides or video. Show off your new service or new capabilities, show your point of view and strengthen the reasons for your guests to work with you rather than your competitor. Another avenue to consider is to hold educational seminars, which would highlight how your firm provides solutions to well-known or recognized problems in your industry.

5) **Amenities.** Make sure the guests feel welcome and thank them for their participation. The little things make a difference when creating an impression. A small parting gift, even if it's a branded item (your brand, of course) is fine, but make it a high quality piece. Make sure there is a place to put coats if it's in the winter, offer umbrella escorts from the parking lot if it's raining, valet parking if you have a city location, and other niceties will make a big difference in the overall impression.

6) **Follow Up.** All the entertaining in the world won't make your business grow (unless you're a caterer) unless you connect with those prospects both at the event and afterward, when they are back in their own environment and in decision-making mode. A nice Thank You note to all attendees with a personal note in each will do the trick, along with a follow-up e-mail later that week,

highlighting some of the advantages and benefits you presented them with at the event should help cement your company in the correct place in their mind for future.

Using events to promote your business and generate new customers is a time-honored tactic that works when you pay attention to the little details and you make it look easy. If you're not comfortable with all this, maybe have a dry run for your staff a week before to work out the bugs before getting in front of customers. In general, quality will show you off to best advantage, so work with the best caterer, best beverage supplier, produce a high quality presentation with some production value and take advantage of the opportunity and follow up, and your business will grow before your eyes.

Spring Tradeshow Season is Coming - Are You Prepared?

In many business verticals, Spring/Summer is trade show season. If your marketing plan includes trade shows for your vertical or peripheral industries, and your booth selections and floor plans are set, now you're facing the task of pulling together a strategy, designing and fabricating a display of some sort, creating collateral and sales support materials, and training staff to get the biggest bang for your trade show buck.

That last piece of the puzzle, staff training, may be the most overlooked and the most mission critical to achieving your goals for each show.

Firms we've worked with treated staff training for trade shows as an afterthought, making seemingly random staff selections, and handing them a brochure and saying "learn this" - not a good idea. Some firms who hire spokesmodels do this, but their goal is different and the model's role is different than a staff person.

If you're going to spend many thousands of dollars leasing floor space, designing and fabricating a custom display, paying staff travel and expense to go to a show and work, feeding them, housing them, and paying expenses for them to entertain clients and potential clients, the people you send ought to at least be proficient enough to maximize the opportunity. Sending the mailroom manager, the receptionist, and two Public Relations people because they are young, unattached, unconstrained and attractive will come back to haunt you when the results for the year's sales come in. You'll have a much harder time justifying your budget for trade shows if you don't show good results. Sending the whole sales team may backfire as well, without at least a few technical people there to answer some of the tougher questions, and some senior management to run the show and meet with those key clients as a show of respect for their past and future business.

Proper selection of a good mix of professionals to man the booth is only part of the equation. Making sure they are all on the same page, with the same message and a similar approach, pushing the same products in the same way, speaking knowledgeably about your products or services, is critical to a good show result. They should all be taught how to use their booth time productively, to make the most of the opportunity, how to engage prospects, how to qualify them, how to screen them, how to steer them to the correct individual internally, how to appear and how to behave when they are "on stage" in the booth.

The other key element of trade show success is the follow-up. Studies by Center For Exhibition Industry Research (CEIR) have shown that nearly 80% of all leads gathered at a trade show are NEVER followed-up. You paid for them, why not use them? When you calculate your cost of acquisition at that trade show for new customers, you'll realize what a gold mine they can be, if you've done your homework and set up a system to make sure the leads generated get followed properly.

Some companies do this extremely well, and they usually let technology do the work for them. I know of several companies that go to shows with a complete set of pre-written e-mail follow-up letters, divided into different levels of interest, different product interests or whatever their scheme supports. As soon as a lead is logged, either from a business card or through the badge reader system, an e-mail is issued to follow-p, send links to the company website, impart additional information, give out coupons, keys to prizes, whatever. Sales people have the opportunity to add personal notes to these, to add specific answers to technical questions. Sometimes these systems are extremely fast – I've received e-mails on my smart phone within minutes of leaving the booth!

Whatever system you employ, make sure the staff is trained to use it, and that they use it often. And remember, it's not usually about quantity, it's about quality. If there are lots of leads, but the resulting sales after diligent follow-up are low, maybe that's not the best venue, and it should be reconsidered carefully for next year's plan. On the other hand, if you only get five leads, but they all convert, your cost of acquisition will be very high!

Trade shows are a lot of work, use a lot of resources, and can be an extremely effective tool for generating new leads and new customers, for polishing your brand within the industry, for launching a new product, or for doing product research. But without a properly trained staff, good follow-up mechanisms, and a solid integration plan, all those dollars and hours are for naught.

Leaving Gold On The Table

For those companies out there who include industry tradeshows in their marketing mix, either on purpose as part of a strategy, or "because all our competitors are there," you are probably leaving a pile of gold behind when you pack up your boxes to go home.

Recent studies by independent national organizations show that very few companies do any pre-show marketing to prospects or clients, and that the number of leads actually followed up after the show is in the single digits!

This type of behavior makes no sense to me, and is creating a case of diminishing returns for the tradeshow industry as a whole and for those who participate in them. If you were to spend millions of dollars on a Super Bowl ad for your company, and then disconnected your phones for the month after the ad ran, you'd consider such behavior ludicrous, wasteful to the nth degree. Yet, that's exactly what you're doing when you fail to broadcast your presence at an event, when you pay dearly to participate; spend thousands on a complex display and related collateral material; spend endless time in meetings reviewing a hundred different types of tchochkes and giveaways; take a week's worth of time from your key sales people, technical people and administrative staff; when you don't get full benefit from T&E, including travel, meals, hotels, cabs and entertainment; and then don't follow up some of the most qualified sales leads and partnership opportunities you'll ever encounter. Absurd, you say? Commonplace, at best, if we're to believe the data. And that's just for one major show – scale that up to include 6-10 shows a year, and you're watching a pot of gold in lost opportunity fly out the window!

So how to you capitalize on all that opportunity? Five quick fixes that will cut waste, provide more value and prevent lost opportunity:

5) **Train and select your on-site staff with care.** Even for a major show, you don't have to send the whole team. While a big group of people all dressed alike trolling the floor and inhabiting the exhibit does have some value, especially in reinforcing your brand, it's a costly and inefficient way to do that, and the job can be better handled by fewer better selected candidates. A mixed bag of junior and senior sales staff, one technical person to act as advisor and closer on

the BIG sales, and a couple of engaging administrative folks to help clean up the loose ends, steer traffic to the sales group and provide coverage. That's it. Train them all to be effective in as many different roles as are appropriate, so there is good overlap, but make sure everyone knows how important this show is to the prosperity of the company, and that all leads, no matter how small or remote, could be important, and are to be treated as such.

4) **Set up a lead *management* system, and use it.** That's not the same thing as renting the capture machine from the show management's vendor. This is a system within the company for qualifying, funneling and following up on leads gathered at the show. Your existing prospect database is a good start, but it's probably not built to handle a big influx of leads in a short time, and likely doesn't have a good qualifying system within it. It should be designed to work quickly, have all the follow-up materials created in advance and be able to customize them to a certain extent for each lead. Nothing is more impressive than having a quick, well-crafted, specific follow-up note waiting for you when you get back to your room for the evening from a vendor you spoke with that afternoon!

3) **Craft an effective pre-show marketing strategy.** If you really want to stand out of the crowd, marketing your presence at the show a couple of weeks beforehand is one of the best ways to do it. You can prompt booth visits, make appointments with big clients or promising prospects who are planning to attend, build attendance in your hospitality suite event, pre-qualify leads, and much more with this simple step. Get access to the registration list from the prior year if it's available and use it repeatedly and effectively. You'll be amazed at the resulting traffic.

2) **Set goals for the show that make sense, and hold EVERYONE accountable for meeting them.** Especially if this is one of many shows you participate in each year, goal-setting will give you some idea of how worthwhile your tradeshow investment is likely to be. It gives you an ROI variable to push back against when making decisions for next year. Make them just barely reachable, and make them finite and quantifiable – "we will contact and follow-up with 25 new prospects not in our current database at this show." Now, it's everybody's responsibility to be familiar with what's in that prospect database, know who the big fish are, and engage everyone in a productive, helpful way to make

that number attainable. It forces a teamwork approach, and keeps down the finger-pointing later if you don't hit the number.

1) **See the show as a triple opportunity and treat it as such!** How many times do you get to be in a room with a huge universe of prospects and customers, prepared, armed and in a selling environment, all in one week, with your best troops in attendance? Not very often, I'll wager. So make that opportunity count. Follow-up religiously, engage every reasonable visitor, invest in some staff training, make the display work for you, make sure it carries the brand well and is easy to read and understand, make sure your staff understands the goals and the importance of the results to the success of all concerned. Make sure that lead management system is working for you, not just making you more work.

You've invested a significant chunk of budget to participate in these marketing opportunities – its up to you to make the investment pay back. Enjoy.

Tradeshows - Make a Commitment, Make It Count

My staff at Granite Partners and I recently attended a tradeshow with a client, in an effort to help him gather competitive information prior to entering a new market for a line of products his company was planning to launch in a few months. We got together prior to entering the show floor, and discussed a specific set of goals and tactics to be applied to our activities during the morning, including observing and asking questions anonymously of the competition, researching potential production partners or related ancillary product partners that worked with our product, finding possible new applications for our product beyond the intended use, and observing the marketing tactics used by our potential competitors.

A tall order, but one that can usually be filled in a couple of hours of strolling the show floor, watching, chatting with vendors, asking questions as if we were in the market to purchase, along with a few covert snapshots of displays and a collection of collateral materials in our show bag.

After spending an hour on the floor, we had accomplished most of the goals we discussed. Some general take-aways on the state of small tradeshows:

1) Vendor displays have gotten less expensive - and less professional. If you're going to spend the time and money to highlight a new product at a tradeshow, don't have your sister-in-law design the booth and the collateral signs because she won Third at the science fair in 11th grade! Go to the professionals for your exhibit design, and have a professional help you with a marketing plan that will help activate and leverage that display and turn it into viable leads! Just because the structure is less expensive than it used to be, doesn't mean you shouldn't spend the savings on good design!

2) If you've gone to the trouble to design and transport a display, at least show up, set up and participate. We saw three or four empty booths, half constructed and missing key elements, with no sales or technical staff in evidence – shame on you, what a waste!

3) If you are prepared and suited up, working the booth, don't just shoot out a generic question to passer-by to try and snag their attention - it's tacky and

worse, ineffective. Simply come out from behind the table, out into the aisle, make eye contact with attendees, and maybe ask a legitimate question, maybe something related to the problem your product solves. If you hit on a sore point, you've hooked them, if that's not their problem it'll be a pretty tough sell to start with and you've not annoyed anyone. Being a tradeshow attendee doesn't mean you've signed up to be molested in the aisles!

4) This is not a re-run of "Boiler-room" – stop trying to close me on a complex, high-dollar, multi-step sale three minutes after I meet you at a show. Ain't Gonna Happen! This is essentially a meet-and-greet with audio-visual support. Simply take my information, give me some data and some salient points that can be beneficial or differentiating for your product, and actually do the follow-up work later in the week. Even at consumer-based, residentially-oriented shows, I may not want to sign a contract on a $10,000 piece of infrastructure construction on my house – such things need researched, discussed with family, budgets allocated, etc. It's a long-term, complex, consultative sale, not a $10 widget that helps wash the car faster.

5) Do some pre-show marketing. Don't rely on the show organizer to do it all for you, your results will reflect such an approach. If you plan to sell into the local market, do some homework, craft a decent direct mail piece, do some segmenting, mail a few key zip codes and let some likely consumers know you're going to be in their neighborhood. You'll be the busiest guy on the floor.

No matter how small a show it is, if you're going to spend the money and time, make it count. Make the commitment, do it 100%, make an effort to be your professional best. If you're counting on a show like this to make your year, your plan is flawed, and your desperation will be readable from a mile down the aisle. A show should be a small part of a more holistic approach to your overall marketing effort, not a make-or-break event.

Tradeshow Promotion Requires Strong Planning

Recently I've been approached by several tradeshow organizers to review, upgrade, or revamp their marketing efforts, for a variety of reasons. With all the visibility and power perceived by marketers who use social media, often tradeshows get put on a back burner. Often there are misconceptions about the cost, value and ROI of exhibiting in a tradeshow, and those impressions are what the organizer is fighting when they try to attract new exhibitors, or build attendance. There are other aspects of working tradeshows into your marketing plan that are misunderstood or poorly perceived that present challenges to the organizers.

Granite Partners has recently been working with exhibitors, and organizers, to eradicate some of these misconceptions, and to maximize the value of the trade-show marketing channel as a viable means of penetrating a new market, launching a new product, or raising awareness of a new application to a new vertical.

When we work with organizers, its often to open up the shows to include new markets, to add new exhibitors and expand the show, or shift its focus. This involves building a strong marketing platform, and a focused sales effort, working in tandem, to approach new exhibitors with a fresh angle or a new spin to show them the value of the show to their sales efforts. Creating a solid prospectus that tells the story accurately and gives the exhibitor a feeling of confidence that the organizer speaks their language, that he understands their market, and that they are competent to make their experience a good, profitable one, is one of the first steps. As always, there's a lot of research involved in creating that element, to gather data on the buying audience, demographics of the attendees, the market as a whole. Once that trust is established, then it's a matter of making contact with the correct individual to work through their issues, concerns and needs to prove to them that the organizer will be with them every step of the way.

When we work with exhibitors, it's usually to help the exhibiting company break into a new vertical market and to make an impact, to raise awareness of their firm within the industry at large. In those cases, it's a matter of getting the attention of the audience, and even of the other exhibitors, be they partners or competitors. Sometimes it's not just a matter of buying a sizable piece of real estate and designing a flashy display. We've worked with some companies where it was appropriate to do exactly the opposite – purchase the minimum size space, install a low-key display, but participate heavily in other parts of the overall marketing opportunity, like sponsorships of events, banners in the halls, kiosks, hospitality suites, press conferences and publication ads in directories, maps and schedules. These kinds of activities require lower levels of human resources, and help present a unified and ubiquitous-appearing presence, while not spending on expensive floor space and having to furnish it with a large staff and display.

No matter who my firm is working with, it all starts with research and planning to maximize the opportunity presented by the show. Solid planning and a knowledge of the audience can make even a marginal show a resounding success, generating revenue, growth and partnership opportunities, and helping markets expand and driving commerce.

Tradeshows Still Posting Good ROI - When Strategically Selected . . .

Below is a posting I thought you'd find of interest . . .

Exhibitions and Trade Shows – A Thing of the Past?
Posted by garethcase · August 30, 2011 · 5 Comments

It's a subject that comes up every year. There is always an Account Manager who wants to do an exhibition because it's closely aligned to their vertical market, but is there still real value in these events?
The internet's exponential growth over the last decade has meant that we have access to pretty much any information we want, no matter where we are or what device we are viewing it on. Research in general, for that latest gadget, your next holiday or even which e-marketing platform you are going to deploy is at our finger tips 24 hours a day.

Before these technological advances, research was the reason I used to attend trade shows, but over the last 10 years, I have noticed a dramatic decline in both the size of events and the number of attendees.

There are many reasons company's {sic} choose to exhibit at trade shows. For example, it's a good forum to launch your brand into a new market or geography. It's also good to have brand presence at an event well subscribed to by your customers. The other main driver is lead generation. How many of you can honestly hold your hands up and say you have had a really good ROI from events and exhibitions overall? I hope I hear about some great successes but in my experience the ROI does not stack up. Yes there have been shows where we have converted some great opportunities, bit If I compare it £ to £ against over marketing activities it probably comes out bottom of the list. When working out the ROI, don't forget to include the investment of time from your employees, a trade show with 4 of your sales team not only means you're paying them to be there, but also missing out on them selling elsewhere during that time.

If you are going to do trade shows and exhibitions then my advice is to pick niche events aligned to specific vertical markets you want to attack, rather that generic shows that cover your solution/product set. The key is to develop a proposition that really helps your target market overcome a 'common challenge'. This way you will quickly gain engagement and been seen as a value add rather than a box shifter.

Surely it's better to be the only company at an event that offers your products and solutions than being one of 150 all offering something similar?

I look forward to hearing your comments on this and don't forget to follow me on Twitter for all my latest thoughts…

My Response:

Gareth – I, too, have sat on both sides of this fence, organizing some of the largest industrial events in the country (US) and attending and exhibiting in hundreds of shows for a variety of clients. I, too, have seen reductions in attendance and square feet sold, likely a factor of a combination of better information sources (the internet and elsewhere) and the current economy. However, if applied to the marketing plan in a focused strategic way, there is still a huge value in live trade events. NOTHING can replace the face-to-face interaction, the energy, the insight gathered at a live event. True, hard data research can be gained electronically, but the "Who" portion of the show is just as important as the "What" that you get electronically – seeing your competitors approach, viewing new entrants into the market for possible partnership, gauging the health and direction of an industry at large, are invaluable to the well-rounded executive.

True, lead generation is one of the principal reasons to exhibit, and many shows don't support this activity aggressively enough, though they should. But on the corporate side, 8 out of 10 viable leads are NEVER followed up with – after spending all that time, money and energy to exhibit, craft a display, man the exhibit with top, expensive sales staff, the leads lie fallow, reducing the ROI by a huge percentage. Shame on the sales manager who lets this practice continue . . .

There are indeed numerous branding tactics associated with a tradeshow outside your individual exhibit, but some of the guerrilla tactics mentioned here in other poster's comments would do more than "irritate the organizers" – they can get them thrown out of the venue, ostracized within the industry, their brand destroyed or reduced to a cartoonish bottom-feeding lout. If you work closely with the organizer, such tactics can be negotiated and usually an accommodation made so that these activities are viable and above-board, and a win for everyone.

The branding aspect cannot be overstated – you're given an opportunity to put your best foot forward in the most prominent arena your company has – a room full of customers and potential customers! Can't ask for more than that in ANY business. When all this is factored in to the ROI equation, a well-selected show that gives you a forum to launch a new product, do primary customer research, show off a rebranding, put on a good face for the industry, and eyeball all your competitors in one room is an unbeatable opportunity. The rumors of the tradeshow's death are greatly exaggerated and superbly premature . . .

Promotional Items Should Be Carefully Selected for Maximum Impact

There are lots of elements to be considered if your marketing plan for the year includes participation in tradeshows, and a number of good reasons to include it in your plan in the first place. One element that has been closely focused on over the years, sometimes to the exhibitors' detriment: the tradeshow "giveaway." The use of promotional items for creating lasting attention and retention of brand image has cycled up and down in popularity over the last 50 years or so. There are some interesting correlations between the state of the economy and the level of quantity and sophistication attached to the promotional items given out at shows. In general, when times get tough, the quantity goes up, and the quality/cost goes down. When times are hard, something in marketers minds says "better to give away lots of cheap stuff just to get the name out there, than to spend the same but only give away half as many nice items that actually connect accurately to the brand". Why, I have no idea, but its bunk.

In reality, if you choose to distribute promotional items at a tradeshow, that choice should be as well-thought-out as the display construction, the sales training scheme for the event, the selection of size and location of the stand, and the selection of representatives working the show. Often such items are an afterthought, an add-on after everything else has been decided. Sometimes, there are "Standard" items that the company keeps a stock of, or makes available to each location for marketing purposes - they get a better price buying in higher quantity, and they make available or distribute it throughout their "system" for use in ad hoc marketing efforts, including local tradeshows. Ever visited a home improvement show, and the local bank has purchased a table space and brings water bottles and stress balls, and thinks this will make them memorable to the attendees and that they will open an account or apply for a loan? For the impact that really has on the audience, they may as well have taken the money and put it in one of those Plexiglas Grab-a-Buck boxes - that at least connects money and banks in people's minds and might have gotten them some attention!

If you've made the decision to promote your business with a branded item, if that selection is made carefully, it can be of great benefit at that event, and can drive recognition and awareness, not necessarily sales. If really obvious, it can create buzz on the show floor and drive traffic to your display from elsewhere on the floor. And if you've really read the audience right, that item will be so specific to a particular population that it will help qualify that traffic and thin and focus the lead selection before they arrive! Now that's a promotion.

Some general rules of thumb for a successful promotional item giveaway.

1) If you can do so, and it's appropriate, try passing out samples of the product. Smaller, not necessarily fully functional, but a good replica of your product will at least remind the recipient for months to come, who gave them that item and what they make.

2) If you can't sample, for whatever reason, select something that links practically to what you do or what you offer. This type of item at least will carry some activation, that coupled with the logo printed on the item, will conjure up a memory of your firm and what it offers.

3)If you can't sample, and you can't link practically with your product, link with the audiences habits or industry specific needs or processes. If you're marketing to engineers, a measuring device of some type is a good example of this - they can actually use the item at work, where they hopefully make purchasing decisions.

4) If you can't do 1, 2, or 3, at least make the item something useful or entertaining and of good quality, including the imprint method. Also, be aware of the audience. If you can, try to select items that are at least non-toxic - sounds strange, but I can't tell you how many stress balls and foam toys I've handed to my young kids only to find out the printing rubbed off when they got drool on it, or put it in their mouths.

In short, smart, engaging, creative choices that engage the audience's imagination, trigger a memory of what you do, your products or your brand promise, that are practical and useful within your industry are the best bets for effective giveaways.

There are lots of other tips and tricks to using promotional items to drive traffic and leads.

10 Things You Can Do To Boost Attendance at Your Next Conference

Everybody likes something for nothing, but most business people have become spoiled by attending meetings and conferences on the company's dime. Well, based on current economic conditions, some of your member's companies may have precious few dimes to spare for sending their employees to meetings, even though they will be the first to admit the value is there and that they support training and education. So, how do you encourage member companies to help their employees further their professional education, and in turn provide increased value to the company as employees? Below are 10 approaches that have found success, under a variety of economic conditions, at putting attendees in their place – at your meeting.

1) Make it Easy

All the conference marketing in the world can fall apart at the registration form if it is too complicated, too difficult to read or understand or if there are too many steps to the finale. Examine your registration form, and if it takes more than five steps to the last page that says "Congratulations, You're Registered," it is too tough, and will likely experience a higher level of abandonment (web or paper), no matter what the price or location. Simplify, Simplify, Simplify (apologies to Thoreau).

2) Help Them Find You

Create a separate landing page for your conference, different from your website – a simple one-page info sheet with a button leading to your registration page – and optimize it for search engines to the very best of your ability. Keep it maintained, keep it fresh as speakers or events are added, and be sure to update and modify the tags to really zero in on the typical searcher – your Internet Service Providers reports should show you where the visitors are coming from and even some information about location, dwell time and other indicators of audience origin. Read those reports, and use them to guide your optimization. If you do not have that expertise in-house, countless Search Engine Optimization (SEO) firms would be happy to help you for a reasonable fee. Use that landing page address on anything not nailed down that goes out of your office – fax covers, e-mail signatures for all staff, all collateral, book and purchase receipts, dues invoices, outer envelopes, everything. Drive traffic there, and the registrations will follow.

3) Help Them Get There

In an era of rising energy and transportation costs, getting to the meeting and staying there are the two largest expenditures for all but the most local attendees. If you can find some way to offset some of those costs that works for nearly everyone, take full advantage of it and promote it heavily. Car rental companies, hotels, airlines, Amtrak, all offer some sort of discount package, and many can be persuaded to start such a program for you if the volume is sufficient to warrant it. If you add up 10% off the car rental, 15% off the hotel room (above the normal block discount), free hotel shuttle to the convention site, possibly a free meal coupon at the convention, and 10-15% off airfare from select cities with a single carrier, that adds up to significant savings. Once these arrangements are in place, promote them heavily, showing how much you've saved your attendees over doing things on their own – you've got to beat the travel aggregators at their own game, and that required a certain level of creativity and the ability to go the extra mile for your members.

4) Keep It Close To Home

Do your homework, and some analysis on your attendance patterns, especially when selecting location. Pull the last four year's worth of attendance reports, and group them sorted by city. Clear attendance patterns related to city of origin should emerge, and you can safely let those patterns guide your destination city selection for several years in advance. If 60% of your members come from the East Coast, and the balance are sprinkled in the Midwest near the Mississippi river, don't schedule your next convention in San Francisco – everyone has to travel to that one, and their costs will shoot up as a result, giving you lower attendance. As a rule of thumb, to avoid location drop-off, no more than 10% of your attendees should have to travel more than 500 miles. Unless you are limited by available venues of a certain size, there should be a suitable location that fits those parameters for the great majority of organizations.

5) Bring the Family

One of the most popular strategies for families who are looking to cut costs is to combine business travel with family vacations, effectively cutting the overall vacation cost by the amount subsidized by the company to send the employee to the meeting. If you facilitate this natural tendency, you will boost your attendance. Make it easy for them by including family activities during meeting hours, offering group discounts for activities, and offering spouse activities including lectures, trips and outings specifically for spouses. Work with your destination cities to arrange for special branded days at local attractions, discount offers for attendee's families, family oriented hotel amenities and the like to encourage bringing the family along. If you offer something of value, they will come.

6) Make It Fun

You know you have great content, and that your meeting is a valuable source of interaction, networking and industry solidarity-building, but all work and no play makes Jack and Jill dull folks. While some groups go overboard by centering the meeting around the golf outing, be sure to find a good balance in your program agenda between educational activities and team-building, lighter and more fun activities. Carefully placed on the seminar agenda, they won't hurt your session attendance, and will increase your overall attendee count noticeably. Be sure to announce the winners of any competitions or contests to the general populace at a time when all can recognize them, to help build participation for this event next year.

7) Show the Value, Not the City

If your meeting provides real value for the attendees, offers features for everyone can find beneficial, and gives your members a way to connect with their peers and colleagues, the city is a distant third on the list of reasons to attend – so why does so much of the current marketing material showcase and theme off of the destination city? Granted there are funds to be had by collaborating with the local Convention and Visitors Bureau to help promote the destination, but that does not mean that the city is going to resonate with your members' needs for a conference. They may have had a bad experience with or in that city, not have reasonably convenient flights in from their home location, or not be much of a draw for a segment of your membership for whatever reason. Why risk alienating a segment of your membership by leading the charge with the city. If you offer good content, your marketing should be able to substitute the city name for any other at will, with no negative effect on offer value, graphic presentation, or registration rate. Take this test: pull your latest conference promotion and substitute Ottumwa, Iowa, for the destination name currently there, and see if your meeting value proposition drops or if your imagery or graphics no longer make any sense. If so, you are depending too heavily on the city's cache to attract attendees, and at some point you will hit a clinker and your meeting attendance will drop precipitously for no apparent reason.

8) Let Them Know You Care

Once you have garnered a registration from a member, that should be the beginning of the conversation, not the end. Keep in touch with your registrants almost as rigorously as you do your prospects, and your no-show rate will drop precipitously, boosting actual attendance. Offer special discounts for registering before a certain deadline above and beyond the usual early bird special. Cut rates for those who register online rather than by mail to encourage online registration. Offer free transportation to the conference venue from a series of destination hotels if they register by a certain date to encourage early registration. The more you over-deliver and under-promise, the more likely they are to actually board the plane and attend, and still feel great about the experience.

9) Let Them Pay Their Way

Make paying for the meeting easy, convenient and reasonable. Allow for the broadest range of payment methods possible, including adding their registration costs to their dues invoice for the year (for a slight increase in price), take all the credit cards you can, accept checks both personal and corporate, offer discounts for multiple registrations on one bill, anything to make payment easy for the attendee. The more open you are to such options, the more likely they will make an effort to find a way to pay you to attend, and the more creative they will be in arranging for that payment. Couched properly and priced correctly, pay-up rates won't suffer significantly, and your attendance figures will rise beyond any additional risk incurred.

10) Let Them Bring Some Moral Support

Flying to a strange city, finding the conference venue, signing up for the "right" seminars, attending functions populated by strangers, and making it home again can be daunting for a certain segment of your membership, especially the newest members, who might not have attended one of your events and don't know what to expect. Increase their comfort zone and reduce their trepidation by offering a reduced rate if they bring a friend or colleague. Traveling together is a great bonding experience and can make things easier, sharing rides to the airport and the venue, attending sessions together and comparing notes, etc. By subsidizing the Buddy System, you have just increased your attendance by 25% but only increased your costs by 12.5% – not a bad formula.

Whatever you do to promote your meetings, boosting attendance year over year will be especially tough when the economy takes a turn into negative territory. The more you are willing to give now the more your efforts will pay benefits when things get better. You will have increased your penetration of your membership, boosted their loyalty, and given them a reason to spread the word to their peers and industry colleagues about the value of your meetings and your organization as a whole.

Chapter Takeaways:

1. Tradeshows have been around for centuries, and they still represent an effective, viable marketing method for businesses of all types. To reap the full benefit of the investment of time, effort, resources and expertise required to use tradeshows as a marketing vehicle, there are some areas that require specific effort.

2. Solid planning and a strong commitment are required to make the most of the opportunity that a well-chosen tradeshow represents. Your participation in it, including the selection of promotional items, should be considered thoughtfully.

3. Tradeshows are one of the people-oriented marketing activities that a company can undertake. Staff training, exhibits and the rest are nearly worthless if there aren't enough of the right types of attendees on the other side of the exhibit table. It requires the right mix of industries, titles, sizes and types of business representatives in the aisles to provide the best ROI.

9) Social Media

Is Social Media Marketing's Magic Bullet?

For the last 18 months or so, Social Media, and the tools through which it is accessed, e.g. Facebook, MySpace, LinkedIn, Twitter and a host of others, have been bandied about the business community as the next big thing. Indeed in terms of public relations "hits" and buzz generation, it certainly would seem that it is indeed the greatest thing since sliced bread was introduced.

But is it all it's cracked up to be in the traditional media? In our work with clients, most when asked have responded that they did indeed have a social media *presence*, but when pressed, they typically didn't have a real *strategy* in which that presence resided. Everyone wants to create a Facebook page, and open a Twitter account, but if you ask them what they expect to get out of it, or why they need it at all, the response is often a blank stare, or worse, a stammering justification that makes no more sense than "Everyone else has one."

Ask the experts in manipulating social media who swim in that pool all day long if they drive revenue for clients, and the response is often a reserved "sometimes." For certain clients, they've been able to score a home run, especially among certain audiences. At some level, everyone who interacts with these programs is a potential consumer of something, and the subtleties of tracking down "influencers" in a given network, identifying them, and corralling them to disseminate a message that will resonate is a real crap shoot except at the highest scientific levels. There is sophisticated software that can make sense of that type of scenario, but the amount of data needed to use it with any accuracy is staggering – well beyond the typical Facebook user's grasp, even for a large enterprise business.

The biggest factor in success with social media seems to be having a sound strategy and having realistic expectations for the results you get – imagine, having a strategy is better than not, who'd have thought . . . . If you think of social media in terms of what you want to achieve with it, and gear your attention and budget toward the realistic expectation of meeting those goals, it becomes clear that you could spend your way broke on time and attention and not get the results you want – just as you can with ads, mail, or any other marketing-oriented media.

If you view social media through the lens of cost per acquisition, it clarifies things greatly. That's a measurable, quantifiable, goal-oriented approach that lets you think dispassionately about the use of the media, and puts it in league with the more traditional approaches for comparison purposes. If it takes six months and $100,000 in salary and set-up costs, and you get 2,000 friends and 10 customers, you've spent $10,000 on each – you could easily improve that number through more traditional means, but at least now you know what works and what doesn't for your particular situation. Test, test, test!

In my view, at least so far, Social Media is a new, trendy way to reach out to customers that does impart some additional power through interactive means, and offers very quick feedback from a self-selected audience (those who have accounts and use the software). Is it the end all and be all of marketing for the next 50 years? Probably not. Not only is there something even newer and fancier coming down the pike by then, but the villains will have stepped in by then and corrupted the use of these tools, and the government will have seen fit to regulate it by then, stripping it of both its novelty and it's power.

Craft a strategy with your eyes open, with realistic expectations, fund that strategy adequately, and your chances of reaping some reward increase exponentially. Analyze your results, make adjustments accordingly, and your chances increase even further. Use it to inform your audience, reinforce your brand, reinforce and augment your customer service efforts and gain referrals and create buzz as a result, and you'll really hit a home run! Use it in conjunction with your overall outreach efforts, not because you feel you should or because everyone else is – Sometimes letting the other guy spend his way through a mistake is a good strategy, too – ask Ronald Reagan . . . .

Barstool Marketing, Part II

So far, I have focused on integrating traditional and web-based marketing using static sites and e-mail. I am sure this would have caused a bit of concern among those who feel that online social media is the greatest thing since sliced bread, since I didn't include social media. There is a good reason for this. Social media is one of those phenomena that have not entirely proven itself in the marketplace as a direct adjunct to direct marketing. It can be integrated with traditional marketing techniques, and has some significant advantages in terms of data gathering and outreach over traditional direct mail marketing. It has different strengths in terms of personalizing and humanizing your outreach efforts, but uses a different mindset for the recipient than more traditional push down or permission methods, and can cloud the issue and actually reduce response if improperly used.

Social media is supposed to involve a conversation, an interactive engaging exchange between entity and prospect. No matter how much you personalize your mail or e-mail, it will never answer your questions, it will never respond to your post, it will never comment or say it likes what you're showing it. That requires a human being. No matter how well-conceived your auto-responder, or your Search Engine Optimization program, or your Adsense server, it's not really a conversation.

Social media has not proven itself to be a reliable long-term lead generator. It can provide customer insights, it can allow you to gather like individuals, build a list, nail down commonality and sense relevance, but as far as generating outright sales on a long-term basis, it has limitations, at least so far. Keep posting messages about a product and see how many you actually sell that can be attributed to those posts – the number won't bear out the expense and effort.

What it can do is allow you to do some solid follow-up and post-sale contact. I got a message the other day from a merchant who had a cookie sender in place for those who clicked "like" on his Facebook page for a particular line of accessories I had visited based on a served ad. It's all web based, with no push other than the fact that I clicked on an ad that was randomly served up by Facebook.

If you sent that in an e-mail or a direct mail postcard, the chances of someone seeking out the Facebook page and clicking "like" is greatly reduced, not only from the media disconnect, but if you've gone to the trouble of finding the Facebook page, or responding to the Twitter note, you might as well search the item and go direct to their main site. That's the only way Granite Partners' consultants have seen among our client base that social media has been effectively integrated - in the after lead or after sale follow-up and cross- and up-sell efforts.

Fully integrated campaigns can and often should have a social media component, to help build an awareness base, drive customer interest, gather data, and keep in touch with existing customers. Driving new actionable qualified leads so far at least should be left to the more traditional approaches.

Who Do You Seek Advice From?

Before all you English majors go off on me, I know the title is making use of poor grammar – but "From Whom Do You Seek Advice?" doesn't really "sing" when used as a headline. 'Nuff' said.

The real question is, how do you select, solicit, and filter advice on the topics in your life and work that matter? Most folks have an informal network of influencers and advisers, people they turn to when they have a question, want to validate a choice or point of view. Some have a small circle, some have a very large network of various family members with a range of levels of expertise. Sometimes it's just that you want to hear another opinion, from someone who thinks like you do, who will dilute and sugar-coat their stance and feed your own back to you, just as a "feel good."

But sometimes, picking the right expert really matters. Sometimes it's a case of hiring a professional who you happen to know under other circumstances. Selecting a realtor, picking a doctor or dentist, finding a tax preparer or accountant, an attorney for non-criminal work – most of those selections are based on referrals or references from our known network of advisers. Sometimes the professional themselves is part of the network! But how do you really make the choice? Is it emotional, is it pragmatic, is it price sensitive, is it strictly relationship based?

Studies have shown that reaching those influencers is the most powerful way to prompt word-of-mouth transference of brand and product information. But how do you find them and reach them? Most of the advisers who are non-family are close friends from various stages of our lives. College roommates, fraternity brothers or sorority sisters, high school buddies, team members from sports activities, vendors of various services we use routinely - familiar faces. To find these people and gather them as a list for someone else is virtually impossible - until now. Social media does exactly that and more. Those influencers and advisers are now called "friends."

That's the real power of social media – reaching the influencers of your target audience. If you wanted to build the killer marketing app, it would be one that selects all the Facebook pages from people that fall into your target demographic based on data presented on the pages, and selects the five most prolific friend commentators that appear next to a question mark. You've asked the audience for help with a question, and those top advisers answer it. Select them and market to them socially, and they will bleed that influence into the key purchaser. We can only dream . . . so far.

For now, we'll have to settle for joining the online conversation in a corporate but personal way, and hope that those influencers see us, hear us, and most importantly, believe us, so that they pass along the attributes we offer to their list of "friends."

Keep at it, the tech geniuses will eventually create the key that unlocks the monetary power of social media, and when they do, look out . . . !

New Trends Not Always the Most Valuable

As a marketing consultant, I tend to observe things critically, find parallels and patterns in everything, to try to make sense of what I see and experience, so I can apply those lessons to client problems. Sometimes that's a good thing, sometimes, not so much.

One morning not long ago, my young son, Alex, was playing in the living room. At 19 months, he sort of wanders around the room, and when his eye catches something bright and shiny or something he remembers from yesterday's play session that was fun, he makes a bee-line for the object, dropping whatever he's got in his hand already. Even though the "old" toy was perfectly captivating just 10 seconds ago, suddenly it's yesterday's news and he drops it like a hot potato in favor of the "new" one.

It dawned on me that some of my clients had exhibited this same behavior regarding their marketing and outreach activities. They were rolling along, sending out e-mail, sending out letters, engaging members or customers with their website, growing steadily, when someone pipes up in a meeting "Hey, why aren't we on Twitter?" or "Why don't we have a Facebook page?"

Before you know it, the whole marketing and Information Technology department is discussing profiles, and launching pages and starting accounts and firewalls and policies and a whole host of related and relevant topics, and before long, these items are in place and being used, to what end no one knows. With all this discussion going on, and activity stemming from that discussion, often there is little or no thought given to integrating this new activity into the existing marketing plan, to setting goals and metrics for those new programs to measure their effectiveness at meeting those goals. Without those elements in place, and really solid and well-researched answer to the questions "Why are we doing this, and how is it going to help us achieve our goals, and how will we know it's working?" – going forward blindly is a recipe for at least needless unproductive activity, at worst brand damage and reputational damage for the company or organization.

Non-profit organizations often have a history of behaving that way, although small to mid-size commercial businesses have been known to do this as well.

They look a lot like my son, tossing aside what's in place, even though it may be working, for the shiny, new, trendy, activity, regardless of its efficacy or effectiveness.

The moral of the story is that while some of the new media channels and applications may look exciting and may be experiencing a groundswell of growth and popularity, it doesn't mean that they are the correct or appropriate types of outreach activity through which to achieve your particular goals. You can spot this type of behavior easily. Simply ask them, "What do you use your Facebook page for?" or "What do you get out of your Twitter account?" It's not even a matter of cost/benefit analysis, it's more about aligning the mission of the organization with the tools and public outreach mechanisms you use to achieve the set goals. Twitter can be a nice, real-time market monitor for short term buzz and brand recognition, even customer service monitoring or public relations effectiveness, but that's more about listening than posting. Facebook can be a good way to build community around a product or service, but it has to be used carefully and with some constraints in place to maintain control of the voice and the brand. It may not be appropriate for it to be used to help drive sales or leads.

If you are contemplating using new media tools, treat them and think about them much as you would any other service purchase - assess the needs, THEN go find the best tool for the job. Don't go looking to add tools when you don't know what the job is. Even Handy Manny knows to use only the right tool for the right job!

Are Accuracy and Grammar Important in The Era of Social Media?

OK, I've about had it with poor language skills being forgiven under the pretext that "as long as you can read it, a few mistakes are OK" on Twitter, Facebook, and LinkedIn.

If Social Media platforms are ever to achieve true legitimacy as a business communications and marketing tool, we have to learn to respect our audience, respect the medium, and respect the message, just as we would any other channel. Would you leave typos and bad grammar in your direct mail, or in a print ad? Production designers, copy writers, proofreaders spend hours poring over copy to ensure accuracy and eliminate errors, and just because it's presented electronically, it's OK to have mistakes published for the public to view? I don't get it, can someone explain to me why this is so?

If these errors, omissions and poor usages are a reflection of the use of language in this country, maybe we should cast a critical eye on the elementary education system. If our kids are being taught that this is the way to speak and write English, then somebody's asleep at the switch and should be replaced. If we as a society condone such poor talent, then we are to blame as well – silence is tacit approval, and as such, saying nothing out of some misplaced sense of decorum is doing us all a disservice.

There are those especially in the previous generation to mine, who value their language, and prize its correct usage and accurate representation. When you read a book or magazine or newspaper and come across a mistake or a typo, doesn't it downgrade your opinion of the whole publication, reducing its credibility, and altering your perception of the accuracy of the information being presented? If they missed the basics, how accurate can their statements or research be?

I wasn't an English major in college, not even liberal arts (whatever that means), but I've had my homework and essays and reports and papers corrected by a professional publication editor according to the *Chicago Style Manual* since I was eight, and after swimming in red ink for years, finally realized the importance of accuracy and correctness in the use of our common language. After a while, the ink started to recede and become rarer, and now with that training firmly embedded, I could focus on the message and how to craft it effectively, and not on the mechanics of producing the work.

If everyone had this level of training (and if our teachers were willing and able focus on it, rather than being glorified babysitters and disciplinarians trying to escape each day with their skins intact, we might manage it), then such things as poor word choice (their vs. there), bad grammar (where are you at), lousy spelling and other grammatical gaffs wouldn't be present or tolerated, no matter who the poster is – it's up to society to set the acceptable standard for word usage and language skills.

It's time to raise the stakes, lower the tolerance levels of bad language use, and revive the love of language that is the hallmark of great civilizations throughout history. From a marketing standpoint, there is potential profitability at stake here as well. Poor language usage and bad grammar are sneaking their way into advertising and marketing copy, television commercial scripts, book covers – the list goes on. Marketing is about impressions, and creating expectations – would you buy from someone who couldn't even care enough about you as a customer to proofread their copy and use the correct spellings? And if they're that lazy and ineffective at communicating about the product, how careful were they when making it in the first place? Not a good message for corporate America to be sending and one that negatively affects the bottom line as well.

The U.S. is already working on becoming a second world nation, economically, educationally, in the areas of business and scientific innovation – let's not add language skills to that list as well.

The World Is More Complex Than What You See on Social Media

In today's hyper-connected, hyper-speed world, our lives, both business and personal, have gotten more complex and more complicated. The two are related but different. Complicated indicates that there are many different aspects, parts, pieces that all have to interact in a specific way to fulfill their desired function. Complicated systems are predictable, and they produce predictable outcomes. A modern airplane has thousands of moving parts and is an incredibly complicated entity, yet its functions are predictable, and it is therefore incredibly safe to use for travel from place to place. Complex, on the other hand, suggests that those many moving parts and connections function in changing ways and allow different parts to interact differently at different times. It is nearly impossible to account for every variable in a complex system, and makes it incredibly difficult to predict, based on a common starting point, the end result.

Social subgroups are complex systems, with millions of interactions all beyond the control and influence of the original starting parameters – it's like a global version of the "telephone" game, where you whisper a phrase in your neighbor's ear, and it goes around the room being passed from person to person, and the final person says the phrase they heard out loud, and everyone marvels at how different it was from where they started. The distortion of the message is caused by variations in the mind's interpretation of what you heard and then repeated, and it broadens the distortion with each exchange until the original is unrecognizable.

Social media works in a very similar fashion – with reposting, re-tweeting, excerpting editing, highlighting and rehashing, the initial message gets edited, distorted, shifted and transmogrified to the point where even if you could attribute it to a real source, it would look quite different than the original. Beyond that, if you use social media as virtually your only input for examples of how other people behave, interact and communicate, it provides you with a distinctly skewed and distorted view of the world as well. There are many who subscribe to the tenet that "if it's on the Internet, or if someone told me that on Facebook, it must be true" much as there used to be those who believed "if it's in the newspaper, it must be true." Electronic social media has gained a level of credibility just high enough to draw in the gullible and provide them with just enough checkable fact that they will swallow whatever they see presented there.

This is an extremely complex world we live in, and information, while moving at the speed of light, is no more credible today than it ever was when it moved by boat across oceans – the source is the key, not the medium. Going viral doesn't make something credible, except by crowd mentality. The fact that two million people read or "liked" something doesn't make it good or true or accurate. It just makes it widespread and popular.

There have been rumors, and indeed deliberate hoaxes perpetrated though and even by the media for many centuries. Even the scientific community is not without its hucksters. Medical quackery, misinterpretation of scientific data, deliberate disinformation, and downright fraud have all been around for a long time, from the earliest days of handwritten books and papyrus, to printed broadsides, radio, TV, digital and Internet websites. Just because your "friend" is behind it, that doesn't make it true or accurate, when the inaccuracy is intentional or accidental.

We can only hope that the next generation learns to moderate their use and understanding and acceptance of media-driven messaging, and that original investigation and research balances off the mindless acceptance of whatever the mass media puts in front of us. If the trajectory of media use today is continued at the current pace, members of modern society will never have to leave their houses, preferring to have all their information served up to them by a select few "content providers" who can spoon feed the public anything they chose with impunity because the curiosity to investigate for ourselves will be truly lost. Pity us if this outcome eventually becomes reality.

Digital Marketing is Direct Marketing in Electronic Clothing . . .

With some prodding from Eric Mohr (http://www.linkedin.com/in/ebm-directmarketingservicesllc)I gave some thought to the reputation of Direct Marketing in the digital age. I read and absorb hundreds of electronic messages every day in the marketing sphere, everything from blog posts to group discussion posts, to e-mails promoting upcoming webinars on marketing topics touting digital marketing techniques, *ad nauseum* . . . !

What that gives me, besides a huge headache from message overload, is a good scan overview of what's up in the marketing space, who's promoting what and what techniques marketers and consultants are using to help their clients succeed (usually). After all that reading, there was something in the back of my mind that bothered and irritated me about most of the promotions and webinar topics – and it finally dawned on me that they looked eerily similar to the promotions and conference topics I was seeing two decades ago pertaining to direct marketing techniques!

Now, don't get me wrong, I understand that the new digital marketing sphere isn't a straight rehash of direct marketing – there are many differences in delivery, technology and targeting operations. What bothered me is the approach that new marketers took, the tone if you will, of the communications, which tends toward the downward focused and toward a certain smug word choice that hit me as an experienced marketer from a bad direction. The underlying meta-text in many of these messages tends toward something like "Gee, you haven't figured out how to use e-mail effectively? We've known about it for a long time, here's what we 'experienced' digital marketers have learned in the last two years."

Guess what, digital marketers, direct marketers who are experienced and have applied their experiences to the use of e-mail, video marketing, targeting and social media, have had it figured out for nearly half a century! There still needs to be a good headline(read: Subject line), the offer has to be compelling to drive response (read: traffic), you can still break up the copy sentence length to help improve readability (read: chunking), you still need to send the message to the 'right' people on the 'right' list (read: geo-tracking for local promotion, keywords and web tracking for global campaigns), and most importantly, you still have to have good data, and use it appropriately, to reach out to the audience, engage their attention, and prompt a response (read: drive click-thru).

Clearly, good Direct Marketing skills, like copy writing, offer formulation, list selection and data mining still have a place in the success of digital marketing, regardless of what the new label for them is. So, why have the large consumer companies tended to gravitate toward the "new digital marketing" agencies to set up e-mail campaigns, social media programs and the like, if those skills reside in abundance at their usual DM agency? Because, like everyone else, hanging the "modern" or "digital" moniker on something makes it the new, shiny, spiffy cutting-edge 'thing', that everybody feels is the magic bullet that will solve their marketing problems. What the digital folks have going for them is the carefully crafted perception that digital marketing is "cheaper" or even "free" compared to all that paper, printing, postage, nixies, Business Reply Envelope accounts, etc., and in some respects that's true. But I don't know anyone who selects a major agency or marketing firm based on whether they use the cheapest methods. They select them based on creativity, skills, and innovation of approach, passion and inspired thinking. So how did the less-experienced (by their own admission and by historical fact) agencies end up capturing this business that the old, experienced guys are perfectly well suited to capture?

Two reasons, I think.

1) **The old guys failed to adapt,** like saber-toothed cats. When digital was developing, these more experienced marketers often doubled down on their traditional skills, beefed up their relationships with traditional clients and grew them, rather than branch out and create digital divisions or think tanks to investigate and develop talent and expertise in those areas.

2) **The younger guys were deeply steeped in computer skills and culture,** and saw the opportunities computers represented based on a comfort with the new paradigm in a very hands-on way. It's a short step from sending e-mail instead of printing and mailing business letters to bulk e-mail and social media promotion, when you already spend a majority of time behind a terminal out of

knowledge and curiosity. If a computer is your greatest tool in life, everything starts to look like a good digital adaptation.

The downside is, much like the shift in the publishing world from printed books and magazines (done by professionals) to desktop publishing in the late 1980s early 90s – having the tools doesn't impart the underlying skills and abilities to make the final product effective. Many a butt-ugly company newsletter was produced by unskilled administrative help, involving many unusual fonts, bad design, poor use of things like bold and italics, bad rules and underlining, and a host of ills that the pros learned to avoid in their formal training. But they could do it cheaper, get it out in 'good enough' form and move on to something else.

Same is true here – the digital guys understand the delivery mechanisms and constraints being used today much better, avoiding spam filters, enhanced delivery, subject lines that conform and pass through firewalls, embedded imagery and the like – but that doesn't make them copywriters, or graphic designers, or impart understanding of consumer purchasing behavior or emotional engagement – ever talked to a computer geek at a party – not the height of emotional involvement in the conversation, was it?

We've got the tools on the digital side that traditional direct marketing could only dream of even ten years ago - the ability to track audiences down to the individual level based on *behavior*, not just transactional history - a huge boon to experienced marketers! Now if we can just get the two camps together, to use those tools effectively based on years of tried and true techniques of engagement, not just delivery, marketing can rise to the level of a pure science and really drive revenue and loyalty like never before - something to put on your Christmas list for this year, gang . . .

Is Facebook Making Us All Victims of TMI (Too Much Information)?

First, let me start off by saying I like new technology. I like advancements and the convenience and ease of life that well-designed technology brings with it, and I like the environment of innovation that gives birth to new things all the time. Technically speaking this is a very exciting time to be alive, and I really appreciate that fact.

However, some new technologies have an unrecognized downside as well, and I think Facebook may be one of those that have a dark side most users aren't aware of. I don't mean to pick strictly on Facebook, its developers have created a very powerful networking platform and grown the user base to pretty substantial numbers in a short period of time. But they are the most visible of the social platforms, ahead of Twitter and LinkedIn and some of the others, so they can take one for the team. Social networking platforms serve a valuable function, in providing ways to connect with others who you may not otherwise have an opportunity to meet. There, I said it, given credit where credit is due.

The downside of this is largely in the form of TMI (Too Much Information). Do I really need to know what you had for dinner last night, and who fixed it, and what it looked like plated? Do I need to know that you're "REALLY busy" and only watched a few minutes of *Dancing with the Stars* last night, or that your kids are waiting for the doctor to see them, or that you read the same article on Kim Kardashian as the rest of the world and posted it here just in case anyone missed it? Probably not. I wouldn't tell some of my best friends things like that, for fear of boring them out of their chairs, let alone broadcast them to nearly complete strangers. If you came up to someone on a bus and showed that person a picture of your dinner, they would likely either want you locked up as a lunatic, or have you arrested for assault. But it's perfectly fine to so electronically and no one complains.

From a marketing standpoint this creates a bit of a dichotomy of thinking. Facebook is facing some serious privacy issues recently, in terms of what it divulges to whom. We're worried about some hacker getting a hold of information like your birthday or your maiden name, but we blast out our schedule of potty breaks, brand preferences on hair coloring, sneakers, flip flops, dresses, and food brands willy-nilly to anyone who will listen. Marketers are getting smarter about using these little tidbits to serve up ads for things we'll find enticing, based on the content we post, as well as the pages we visit, and the keywords we use. If you think that posting 30 pictures of your pug isn't going to lead to you receiving ads for dog food, vet services, medicines, toys, leashes, poop bags and a host of other dog-related items in the months to come, you're still living under that mossy rock Ugg the caveman used to hide himself from the world.

Social media has many positive and well-meaning attributes, but there is a downside to making all this mundane information public. You're friends know EVERYTHING! You haven't left much to talk about when I can track your schedule on a day-to-day basis, know your kids meal schedules and doctor appointments, your vacation plans and which words you bid on Words with Friends. I can pretty much fill in the blanks myself without ever talking to you - ever. The security aspect alone is enough to scare you - home invaders take note: "I'm going to be away in Disney World with little Johnny's Cub Scout Troop 349 from May 27 - June 4" – thanks for being neat, guys, make sure you turn out the lights when you leave . . ..

By all means, continue to be "social" digitally, but be smart about it. Maybe give some thought to how valuable is that content I just posted, and how else can that information be used . . . it might save you a lot of grief, and will certainly leave me an excuse to call and talk to you on occasion, find out how you're doing . . .

Buzz Word . . . Meet Social Media

Marketing has long been the point of origin for jargon and buzz words, some of which have become legendary, but in a bad way, from over- or misuse. Management books used to be rife with such dreck as well, and still are, but they tended to be corralled by the selective size of the audience – only so many folks are going to read management books and repeat what they read in public, and the ears these fall on are usually attached to those who also read the same book – self-limiting the damage. But, as you've heard me opine in the past, "everyone can 'do' marketing" so the audience for such buzz-words is by definition larger and the pass-along rate exponentially faster.

Well, now the jargon monsters have discovered the Internet, specifically social media platforms, and the forums, chat rooms and discussion boards are just brimming with buzz-words, accelerating the already speedier-than-light transmission of such junk words as "brand-engagement ambassador," and "batch-and-blast" e-mail tactics. At the 10,000 foot level, marketing is fairly simple: identify potential customers, find a way to show them what you have to sell in the best light possible for them, make what your selling available, and deliver on whatever promises you made in Step Two. That kind of activity really shouldn't have to develop a huge specific vocabulary in order for practitioners to communicate effectively. But it has. Marketers being marketers, anything that shows how clever we are, how difficult our job is, and in reaction to that sentiment I voiced earlier that "everyone can do this", is going to generate a certain amount of complexity and job security that comes with the development of a somewhat murky vocabulary. Lawyers have done it for centuries, as anyone who's read the mouse type on the back of an airline ticket can attest. Job security and exclusivity through jargon and obscure language development is a time honored tradition.

Buzz-words crop up in the most unusual places sometimes. I heard someone at a professional luncheon the other day ask a question that was so packed with jargon and *non-sequitur* word strings that I couldn't understand what he/she were asking . . ... The speaker did a good job of covering that he didn't get it either, mostly by firing back his own barrage of buzz-words faster and louder. For communications professionals, we're doing a lousy job of telegraphing ideas from one person to another when that happens.

Teenagers who use the phone like an extension of their psyche and broadcast their every thought and deed to their friends use a lot of jargon, abbreviations, buzz-words and other communications short-cuts, in some cases to encode their communications to make them intentionally exclusive of adults who might get hold of the device while they sleep (the only time they let loose of the things, and sometimes not even then). These new language tools develop quickly and spread even quicker, in today's hyper-connected world. What's "cool" to use one day is "out" the next, and they've moved in three new phrases or abbreviations to replace it. In some cases these are good things, functionally as they save on verbiage in a character-sensitive communications platform like texts or Twitter, but in terms of language purism, they degrade basic communications skills, and limit the ability to communicate outside the included community. And this is where marketers are going to run into a problem. If the buzz-words start to outrun the ability of the non-marketing audience to understand them, they lose their power to persuade, and overuse only worsens the problem.

I've commented elsewhere in this book on the need for marketers to preserve and cultivate credibility, in order to earn respect that the practitioners of the profession deserve. Having the audience tune us out due to lack of understanding of this weird language we've developed to try and keep our jobs and justify our salaries is counterproductive to that goal, and works to everyone's detriment. If we were half as clever at developing new approaches, at working with the language we have to master the craft of communication and persuasion as we are at creating new ways to show how clever we are, we'd be way ahead. Spend less time preaching to the choir on social media forums and remember those famous words, "Go sell something." Got to go boost my Klout rating and engage with my daughter's brand potential . . ... For more buzz-words, see this great article: http://blog.hubspot.com/blog/tabid/6307/bid/31068/31-Fluffy-Buzzwords-Marketers-Overuse-and-Abuse.aspx/?utm_medium=social&utm_source=twitter

Emoticons Do NOT Elicit Emotion from Prospects

I have gotten several e-mails and text messages recently from other professionals and colleagues that contained one or more emoticons – you know, those little symbols of smiley faces or their derivatives made out of punctuation marks. These have become more popular with the advent of phone texting and Twitter, platforms of communication which limit the character count of a message. They are safe little familiar symbols that can be used in informal, personal communication to convey mood, or indicate that the preceding message isn't serious. But one of the messages I received was acting in a different role, that of a selling communication piece, and I felt it was inappropriate to include this little symbol in this message. It reduced the seriousness of the document, as it was intended, but it also reduced the credibility of the sender, and diluted the sales message to the point that no serious prospect would consider buying services from this company – a net loss just for using a little symbol.

That shows the power that written communication still has to hold, engage and persuade us in today's high-speed communications environment. It also shows how much impact a few characters can have, be it negative or positive. Written communication is one of the elements that separates Man (big M) from other animals, and as such, I feel it's owed a certain level of respect and that each of us should practice it's usage and strive for the highest level of clarity and effectiveness in all of our written communication efforts, no matter how trivial or insignificant it's intent. These little symbols work against that principle and as such have no place in professional communications.

Language is a very powerful tool, and written language has the additional advantages of thoughtfulness and permanence. You can take your time, craft effective phrases, get the word choice exactly correct to convey slight shades of meaning, and one you write it, either on paper or on a screen, you can review it again and again, in different contexts and under different circumstances, to help digest and grasp the intended meanings over time.

Professionals, like the consultants here at Granite Partners, spend hours and hours honing their writing skills, crafting effective copy that evokes an emotional response from the reader, one that can persuade the reader to take action, either in advertising, or in direct mail, to make a purchase, to send back a coupon, to answer a survey, to buy an ad, and a host of other activities, without using one of these little symbols. We spend days devising questions to elicit a usable response in surveys, either to be spoken or read by the respondent, and don't use any of those little symbols. We spend hours on the wording for a headline that elicits just the right emotional response, days on a piece of collateral material, fact checking, spell checking, organizing and editing to elicit just the correct reaction to the offer and call to action – without using any of those little symbols. So why are they even here?

People use them in personal written communication as a short cut. They are lazy, or not properly motivated or sufficiently educated to use their own language properly, so the symbols make it easier to convey emotion with a limited vocabulary. This type of symbology works well for public signage, to convey information without the language barrier, in the interest of safety or order. However, it's not appropriate for business communication, marketing copy, formal communication of any kind. They create a negative connotation for the reader by rending the power from the carefully chosen words preceding them.

It may seem curmudgeonly to professional readers, but I feel that anyone who has graduated with a diploma from a public high school paid for by tax-payers in the country should be able to craft a sentence that is adequately robust so as to not need to add an emoticon at the end to convey meaning. Maybe a little test about a week before graduation for every senior, one that asks each one to write five paragraphs that will be sufficiently eloquent to persuade the principal that they should be allowed to graduate, without using the little symbols. I wonder what that would do to summer-school enrollment . . . ?

Does Social Media Marketing ACTUALLY Drive Customer Behavior and Convert to Revenue?

Social Media, social media, social media – there, I said it three times into the mirror, now I just have to wait and see what happens . . .

That seems to be the approach many companies are taking to this relatively new phenomenon. The head in the sand approach might have some advantages in the long run, if recent data on the effectiveness of social media in driving customer behavior is to be believed. It seems that despite all the hype, and press, and *sturm-und-drang* in the digital media, minting new "social media gurus" by the flock, digital media and it's permutations don't drive near as much revenue or even shopping behavior individually than they do when used together. Integration seems to be the real strength behind conversation marketing's mechanics, and when the reams of data generated are used properly ACROSS multiple platforms, it seems to at least have the ability to drive a solid promotional campaign and boost response levels.

That said, here are some interesting tidbits of data, excerpted from a recent Gartner Group (a well-respected professional market research firm) study:

- 11% of polled consumers had read a company blog, and only 4% had commented on one.
- Twice that many, or 23% had viewed a company provided video.
- 45% said they planned to purchase based on a combination of brick and mortar, digital ads, and mobile marketing, but only 1% said they planned to do so based on mobile marketing alone.
- Only 26% of consumers said they had clicked on a Search Results page paid ad - irrespective of engine brand.
- Based on data from another similar study, only 6% said they had purchased based on a Facebook ad
- 40% said they had registered for a promotion or contest based on an e-mail or social media ad

Clearly, consumers want something for nothing (hence the contest results), but don't want to work at it (read the blog data, reading a whole blog takes effort)

Also just as clearly, mobile marketing has not reached the level of credibility, trust or penetration it's purveyors would have you believe, and while it may be the next big thing, it ain't there yet, not without massive support from other media to reinforce its message and bolster its credibility.

Video seems to have made substantial inroads, but anyone who recognizes the level of involvement the TV generation needs to engage will see a clear correlation between the aging of the boomer TV generation and the level of importance video has attained. Add in the near ubiquity and availability of high-speed broadband Internet access allowing for video transmission at better fidelity and faster speeds, and video's effectiveness becomes less mysterious. The fact that consumers would rather watch a video and have their eyeballs babysat rather than read and understand and digest and analyze a company blog to get their information is less than mysterious as well, when the audience is considered.

The trick with all this is to take the data it generates, and use it to form better customer profiles that can be used to not only drive behavior, but to predict it as well. If you can create a digitally integrated campaign that uses the initial brush with consumers to link to a behavior and transaction based profile, you can then draw that consumer along a continuum toward a purchase after several touch points are hit. That's how integration beefs up the ROI equation. The development of such campaigns requires broad and detailed knowledge of the target audience, so that it can be set up to account for the wide variety of behaviors possible by consumers. If you can narrow the range of preferences and behaviors, and drive consumers down a narrower funnel, the ROI can be quite lucrative.

According to Gartner, "Companies using in-bound and event-triggered marketing techniques to draw consumers will see a 600% higher response rate compared to traditional outbound push campaigns." That sounds pretty fantastic. I wonder if that will continue to be the case as more firms start to embrace this practice and it becomes more common. Will this type of campaign reduce the level of trust and credibility across the board, making consumers more distrustful? Interesting to ponder, but I think not. To paraphrase W.C. Fields, "no one ever went broke underestimating the gullibility of the American public."

Chapter Takeaways:

1. The rise of social media platforms is a digitally derived evolution in the communications process. It is symptomatic of society's need to connect and still maintain control of their personal interaction, coupled with the need to be noticed and popular with their fellow humans, by whatever means necessary.

2. Marketers should view social media as another communications channel, a tool available to them to help fulfill their outreach mission, along with any other appropriate means they can devise or justify to get the job done, not as a magic bullet that is all you need to effectively market products and services.

3. There are subsets of social media, and as no standard for any of these communications platforms have been generated on a global basis, it's pretty much the wild, wild west in the digital sphere, where anything goes until someone makes a rule against it, a constantly evolving methodology for reaching out and connecting to subsets of the population which have been deemed desirable.

10) E-mail

Read Twice Before You Hit "Send"

Everyone makes mistakes – I don't care who you are in life, you've made a mistake or two along the way, its virtually unavoidable. In fact, making mistakes is often the hall mark of successful individuals – you learn more from making mistakes than from succeeding the first time out. The real trick is not only to learn from them, but also to avoid making them in future. Making the same mistake multiple times shows a lack of self-understanding, wondering why things go wrong as a result is the definition of insanity!

One mistake I see many younger business associates make is to put something in writing and deliver it to a recipient before reading it and considering the impact on the recipient later. In the old days, if you had an unfortunate experience or got caught in some less than optimal circumstance, you could fire off a letter to the one who initiated this slight, real or imagined. This involved sitting down, composing the thought. Then you had to find a piece of paper, an envelope, a stamp, and physically write the vehement tract in longhand, place it an envelope, seal it, stamp it, and post it. All this took time – time to consider, reconsider, and with that many steps, many chances to halt the process, and reduce or avoid the impending damage altogether. It took effort to vent on paper, and usually only the intended recipient got to see the result.

Today, with the advent of e-mail, the opportunity for electronic lunacy looms large. Many people spend entire days tucked safely behind a computer terminal, reading, texting, tweeting, e-mailing, posting on social media sites – communicating to be sure, but communicating what? It's now much easier to fire off a venomous missive at the drop of a hat, with no real editor involved, either internal or external. A few keystrokes, a few clicks of the mouse, and off it goes, wounding and excoriating all in its path. And, in true millennial fashion, once it's out there, it stays there. It resides on at least two server drives, yours and theirs, as well as all the one's in between, and can easily be forwarded, used as *de facto* evidence, either for the authorities or in an internal investigation. And, it carries with it an IP address that leads right back to you – no such thing as an anonymous e-mail hate letter.

Even routine business correspondence sent to the wrong place or copied to the wrong address can cause trouble. A quick note to a co-worker about what a jerk the boss was in today's meeting (a bad idea to begin with; never commit such things in writing, it will always be read by the wrong person eventually) can easily end up in the wrong hands with a simple click that's a bit quick, thanks to automatic address lists, group e-mail, and a host of other technological corner-cutting to make our electronic lives even quicker and easier.

To avoid all of this, there are three simple rules:

1) Read all e-mail at least twice before sending, starting with the subject line, word by word, slowly and carefully.
2) If you wouldn't say something to a person's face, don't write it in an e-mail, tweet, Facebook post or Instant Message.
3) Check all e-mail addresses carefully, and verify before hitting "send"

Take a moment, think about what you're writing, think about the impact it can have on other's, and ask yourself what you would do and how you would feel if you received this message in your in-box. If there's any way your message could be taken the wrong way, misconstrued, misinterpreted or taken the wrong way, edit, edit, edit. It's free, it's fast, and can save you hours of grief and tons of trouble later. Thirty seconds of review now can save hours of explanation and hard feelings later, not a great bargain if you ignore it.

E-Mail Effectiveness Boosted by Data Availability

How many e-mail messages do you get every day? How many do you really read? How many get discarded based on the sender alone? Note how the numbers indicate a trend?

I receive at least 100 on most days, 80+ get discarded based on who sent them, even if it's something I've signed up to receive! I just don't have time . . .. The other 20 go to the preview screen for a quick glance, and the top 10 of those get read and responded to that day at some point. Here's five tips for making it to that Top 10:

5) **Make Sure Your Subject Line Has Some Relevance To Me.** Aside from what the excellent spam filter dumps off, subject lines with words like NOW, FREE, TODAY float through here and the urgency is not as desperate as the author would like. Worse are the ones who feel that I need their software so badly and that it's so present and ubiquitous in my mind space that you can open up with the inside jargon and terms you've coined in your dorm room right at the get-go, and I'll know what you're talking about – NOT RELEVANT.

4) **DON'T Waste My Time.** If your subject line is intriguing enough for me to open in preview, be sure you've got something to say that I can understand at a glance – if I have to go to five links to get the info I need, we're both wasting time - you by writing e-mails that are more complicated than they need to be, you might just as well send me the series of links with no text – the result is the same: DELETE.

3) **If You've Got a Good Headline, Don't Bury it in the Image Art, Because I'll Never See It.** Thanks to the preview screen and firewall software, along with Microsoft's inherent wisdom, anything with an image is held back until I purposely ask for it, to save me from intrusion and overuse of bandwidth. If you put your headline in the image, I see a blank white box – DELETE! Any hope you had of that long-worked-over and clever headline grabbing me are immediately gone.

2) **If You Can't Use the Data You Have Correctly and Clean Your List Completely, DON'T USE IT!** I get mail addressed to one of the many websites

I have currently live, about various things, but they assume that putting the web address in the subject line will peak my interest, but the subject or offer have nothing to do with the website they're using to "get to me". My favorite is the Chinese granite counter top purveyors sending me offers of cheap product, thinking I'm a contractor or granite wholesaler, based on the name. They did a search for the word Granite and scatter-gunned an e-mail out to the whole results list – the Doctor says: DELETE

1) **If You Have My Name on Your List, Use it Correctly - Get Your Technology Act Together.** I can't tell you how many e-mails I get with the wrong gender, the use of both names in the wrong order "Dear Poulos, David" and other idiocy of technological laziness. Don't let the 'chines ruin your marketing program, proofread your list! Some simple data processing, at roughly $1 a name or less, all told, will avoid all this and make your list much more useful, to boot. Be a professional, spend a little money, and watch your response rates skyrocket! It's my name, I've had it for decades, you don't think I'm going to find it first and check that you're legitimate by its use? DELETE!

E-Mail Makes A Comeback . . .

There was a time, not too long ago, where marketing pundits and other "experts" were saying that E-mail had run its course as a marketing media vehicle, that it was stale, that it's open rate was too low, that the spam filters and firewalls had made it nearly impossible to get good results with e-mail marketing.

Now those same pundits have to eat their words as major marketers are singing the praises of a well-crafted, simple e-mail to your hottest, most worked on lists. As usual, it's the message, not the medium that counts, and a well-crafted effective anything will always beat the schlocky, hacky, abusive e-mail campaigns that desensitized audiences and killed response rates based on misuse and abuse of the medium and therefore the audience.

As always, it comes down to personal approaches, real, workmanlike copy, free of typos, grammatical redundancy, slang and other silliness that kill credibility. E-mail is still mail, and it's still sent to a single address, which means there's a person on the other end. Simply write with that person in mind, on a one-to-one basis, and suddenly watch open rates soar, response rates double or triple, and sales shoot skyward.

Never mind all the gimmicks, bells and whistles. I know of one marketer that sends out plain text stuff that nets him phenomenal response rates – not a photo to be seen, not even a logo, just good effective copy, real headlines that resonate with the audience – his secret? He writes to his Grandmother in his mind – if the offer is clear enough for her to understand, if the copy clean enough that she won't cringe (Grandma was a Junior High English teacher), if the intent clear enough and the benefits plain enough for her to like it, he's got a winner. Yes, he primarily markets to an older audience – but these days unless you work for Disney, who doesn't? Not a bad acid test – can you latest missive pass it?

Keep it simple and keep it direct – speak to a specific person – if you personalize, be sure to get their name and gender correct, otherwise don't bother. Nothing will kill response quicker than the feeling that you didn't even care enough to send the right message – it's like reading someone else's mail, and it creeps people out.

Keep the file small, keep the message simple – huge files still give viewers trouble, big images still get caught in spam filters and firewall screeners. The trend in design these days is to make the whole e–mail an image or series of images – and my browser is set to make me actually request these image files in order to view them – why make me work to see your information? It would have to be a heck of a headline to make me click three more times and wait for them to load, when I can simply hit "delete."

A well–researched list is still the key to success with E–mail. Most rented lists under-perform, as e-mail addresses change more frequently than physical addresses. A self-selected list is best – based on a web login, or a previous response, or an inquiry, something you can verify and be sure is "opt-in" work very well – permission marketing is still king!

Frequency is something you can debate all day, but suffice to say if you irritate your audience, your response will drop, and often less is more. I'd rather hear from you four times a year with relevant info than 8 or 12 times with fluff and nonsense. Save it for the good stuff, if you're going to go to all the trouble to put together the mechanics of an e-mail, it might as well be a good one . . ..

E-Mail: B-to-B Marketing's Secret Weapon

At Granite Partners, we use e-mail for a number of purposes, both for our own marketing efforts and on behalf of clients or as part of their plans for growth and retention. I've always thought it was a very flexible, very effective medium when used properly. Unfortunately, some among the marketing community have overused, abused and hijacked this wondrously inexpensive way of reaching out to customers, prospects and others in a personal, accountable way, and given it a bad rap, not to mention fatiguing the general public somewhat, and cutting open rates.

A good copywriter, with a good list and reasonable data skills can make tremendous in-roads using e-mail in several ways.

Outreach

Creating a small community of purchasers or converting good warm leads into sales is what makes e–mail shine. It's personal, it's flexible, it can carry text, graphics, imagery, color palette, brand, everything you need to reach out to your audience, qualify the top responders, and keep providing them reasons to buy. It's also fast, and fairly innocuous – if you receive one and it's not for you, simply delete it – no waste, no environmental impact, no anger necessary. It's also fast! You can get an e–mail campaign planned out, written, tested, set up, and sent out in a matter of a few hours at fastest, maybe a day or two if you have more elements to put together.

Customer Relationship Building

Now that you've created your own little "community" of customers, extending, building and broadening that relationship is a task that e-mail does very well, and most of it can be automated. Small shops, service-sellers and sole proprietors can keep in touch, spread the good word and keep customers up to date on changes, new offerings, schedule changes and availability changes, discounts,

and a host of other semi–transactional communications with customers, keeping your brand top-of-mind, up-selling, cross-selling, incentivizing referrals
and keeping your relationship alive and active, which directly contributes to
the top-line, and moves the bottom line in a positive direction. What's not to
like? These types of activities used to take hundreds of hours a year, and the
scope and frequency was limited. Now, not only can these messages be automated to be triggered in response to a contact, a purchase, a query, whatever,
but they can also be tracked, quantified, monitored, measured, and the data can
be sliced and diced any number of ways, letting you constantly test, tighten and
improve your outreach and customer contact far above and beyond what used
to be possible.

Prospecting

For those folks who've never heard of you, imagine their surprise when they
hear from you not once, not twice, but weekly for a couple of months, each
time refining and improving the relevance of the message until curiosity gets
the better of them and they open and read your mail – score! Cost? No more
than a phone call with a bad script, and more effective then you can imagine.
According to Marketing Sherpa, (an industry leading marketing content website) 85% of CEOs have an expectation that e-mail will increase lead conver-
sion/sales revenue, when only 65% of them put those goals as a high priority.
In nearly every category, and there were 10 in total, e-mail beat expectation of
CEO's in terms of meeting business goals for which it was used. I can't think of
any other medium that can boast that kind of success rate and still stay under
the radar!

Used thoughtfully, correctly, and politely, e-mail can carry the day for marketers, both B-to-B and consumer, at a lower cost per customer acquisition than
almost anything else other than social media, and is more accountable and more
directed that even the most powerful platform out there. Let's hope the abusers
have moved on to something else and e–mail can return to business of business
as we move forward in the new economy. Now, if we could just find a better
launch pad than Outlook . . . .

More Isn't Always Better . . .

How many of you receive more than 200 e–mail messages per day? How many of you receive more than 50 text messages per day? How many of you read more than 200 entries on social media platforms per day? Add to that radio and TV messages, Internet pop–ups, banner ads, product packages, direct mail promotions and other "input" and you have a perfect recipe for sensory overload. Studies have shown that while most people think they can multi–task well, nearly all of them showed reduced focus and performance standards on tests that required them to concentrate on as many as three tasks at once. The tasks got completed eventually, but not always with the level of quality required, and in approximately the same amount of elapsed time as would have passed if they had done each task individually in serial fashion. So where's the gain?

With that many messages coming into our consciousness, none of them receive the attention they deserve, to the point where we actually spend as much energy prioritizing them as we do comprehending them and acting upon them.

Too many choices, too much information, not enough filtering or discrimination between input sources leads to inaction, dilutes the impact of each message, and slows progress and productivity. As marketers, we need to constantly be aware of the environment in which our customers and prospects function. Bombarding them with messages doesn't necessarily lead to action, but does lead to saturation, and that saturation point is far more quickly reached today than it was even two years ago.

That's actually good news for intelligent marketers. It means that spending more money on higher insertion frequency, broader media buys, longer ad schedules, and higher print and circulation runs won't get the desired results, and that knowledge allows us to focus on greater message positioning, greater relevance, tighter targeting, higher impact, and better value in our communications. Less is more, and better is less.

Make it perfect, make it relevant, make it resonate, make it accessible on many platforms and through many channels to allow for preference, but don't bombard or carpet–bomb in order to achieve penetration – the shields are up and it won't work!

Spend the savings in increased production value, higher creativity, better thought processes, higher levels of innovation, originality and transparency – it will pay off ten-fold in the long run.

E-mail Tips for Increased Success

5 Elements of Effective E-mail Messaging

1.   **Carry the Brand** – if you send an e–mail to a new or known constituency, no matter what's in the body of the e–mail, if it doesn't get opened it's a waste of time, and if you don't have your brand prominently displayed, your chances of an "open" are decreased by 70%. Security concerns are at such a level that if you don't recognize the sender, it will NOT get opened. Make sure your "from" address is the one the recipient will recognize. If you're sending through a third party e–mail service, which most will be for lists of any size, be sure they have created an outgoing box your audience will recognize.

2.   **Make the Subject Compelling** – in the inbox or in preview, even on mobile devices, the subject may be the only thing your recipients will see. If you get it wrong, it's irrelevant, looks promotional or like a scam or come–on, it won't get opened. Give the receiver a reason to read further, make it relevant and within your brand characteristic list. Then it reflects accurately and well upon your effort.

3.   **Make it Personal** – Modern e–mail technology allows for multiple personalization of e–mail messages – use it. Sending e–mail that looks like a static ad says to the recipient "you don't know me." You do know them a little so show that you not only know but have something you think they would find of value. Call them by their name, use their company name, pitch it to their gender, include a neighborhood fact – all this comes from just the address block on a mailing list! Make the technology work for you.

4.   **Get it Up Front** – Structure the message like a press release – put the most relevant information in the first few sentences, front load the offer, use a coherent and attention getting headline and subhead. Pique the reader's interest, get him to read further, and draw them in with relevancy. Most people, if they open your message at all, will only read the top 10% of the message before deleting. You only have a few seconds to get your point across, so make it short and sweet.

5.   **Make it Easy to Respond** – One of e–mail's main advantages are the links to web content you can include. Whether it's to drive web traffic, drive donation, registration for events, make it a simple single click to get them the relevant information you wish to convey. Multiple links should be part of the body of the message, as well as at the bottom where the response mechanism is likely to land. Converted links are fine so that the message makes sense even when printed, and avoids long URL addresses that interrupt the flow of the message. Provide links in multiple formats, both full length and blind as part of the call to action, so that if it gets printed and passed along on paper, you can at least type the URL into the browser and reach the response page. Devise a specific landing page, so that the link takes them to the specific response you want, and they don't get lost among multiple pages of your site.

List Hygiene – Essential elements for high deliverability

Keeping your e–mail list clean and functioning has many advantages, both reputational and economic. There are many parallels between snail–mail mailing lists and electronic mailing lists. The ISPs function in the Post Office role, and they have their rules of conduct just like their paper corollary.

Several rules will help you keep the list clean and effective, now and into the future.

1.   **Respect Your Recipients** – when bouncebacks and requests to unsubscribe should be respected and acted upon immediately. All "Unsubscribes" should be scrubbed prior to the next mailing. Bouncebacks should be examined to determine the reason and a decision made whether to repeat them or drop them immediately. Remove any duplicates – they may not appreciate your message once, they sure don't need it twice.

2.   **Respect the System** – ISPs are duty bound by their customers and enrollees to police their bandwidth and protect their customers. Repeatedly mailing to bad addresses will alert the ISPs and your mail may be considered SPAM. Set up feedback loops with the ISPs to have them alert you to requests

to stop mail and other dead ends in your list. Take your bounceback that are bad links and use them as the seed of a suppression list for future mailings.

3. **Check it on the way in and the way back** – use data checkers in your data entry screens to keep out obvious errors and fat–finger mistakes – simple things like seeing the "!" in place of the "@" can raise your deliverability. Check the bouncebacks for simple errors and correct them immediately, especially errors in the domain name, which can be done with a find/replace algorithm.

4. **Take out the obvious offenders** – remove all addresses that have the word "SPAM" in them, and distribution addresses – sales@domain.com or info@domain.org – those folks didn't give you permission to reach their entire sales department, and will view your mail as spam and report it to the ISPs as such. SPAM addresses are likely traps added by the ISP and will land you in trouble quickly.

5. **Routinely Revive your Opt–in** – once you have permission via opt–in from a recipient to send something to them, don't count on them remembering that they granted it. For regular e–mailers, those with periodicals and times messages, refresh your opt–in message and take the opportunity to show any value–adds that make it worth it to grant permission.

If your lists are large, some mechanical assistance might be in order. LeadSpend recently introduced a new email validation service that correctly verifies over 97% of all email addresses. Check it out here http://www.leadspend.com/validation . Companies like FreshAddress and others can do some of the hygiene for you and keep your reputation clean with the ISPs.

Mechanical Considerations

1) Make sure your HTML and other formats are readable by ALL formats of e–mail reader, including Outlook and others. If using a service they will likely ask for three versions of the e–mail, one for each of the two major formats and a plain text version.

2) Don't count on an image to tell the story, use text as well. Some mail programs are programmed to strip out the images, or deny your message entry as a result of containing the image, so the recipient never sees them. Some very strict firewalls will deny any e–mail with any images in them at all.

3) Give your audience a chance to unsubscribe – always. If your content is relevant, they won't take advantage of it, and if it's not, you won't waste money on sending to them in the future.

4) Provide a phone number – some people still aren't comfortable spending via the web, but will gladly give out their credit card number over the phone, thinking it's safer.

5) Make sure the links and phone numbers are current and functional – enough said.

6) Test color – some colors read strangely on different monitors and different graphics cards.

7) Keep fancy backgrounds and images sizes to a minimum and still maintain quality – if the e–mail is a huge file it might get filtered out of many firewalls based on size.

8) Make the headline tell the tale – some readers don't get past the top three inches of the screen.

9) Format for mobile – most don't do that yet, and you'll gain an advantage over them if yours is readable on a Blackberry or iPhone.

10) Learn from your mistakes and READ your metrics report from the ISPs and your service provider – there is a lot of valuable information that can be gleaned from open rates, dwell times and other statistics, ready to be used when you design the next campaign for this same audience.

Chapter Takeaways:

1. E-mail communications have not only replaced a grand percentage of typical traditional business communication, it has been adopted as an effective marketing vehicle, a mass communication tool, a security device, a vehicle to share photos, stories and the like with family and friends, even a way for those with physical handicaps to remain functional and productive.

2. E-mail offers some advantages over traditional paper correspondence, including speed of transmission, reliability, trackability in some ways, and ability to act as a vehicle for all sorts of digital information including photos and images, video footage, links to other information, and more.

3. E-mail has some specific requirements when used in marketing, to insure deliverability, and to increase the response rate over traditional direct mail. Those mechanical requirements should be adhered to for optimal efficiency and highest cost/value ratio. E-mail can be effectively used to test marketing concepts inexpensively, and the transmission mechanism actually provides measurement statistics to the mailer to assist in this process.

11) Final Words

For those of you who cheat, and skip to the last chapter of books to see how it comes out, here's the scoop:

Marketing is a combination of art and science. Research and response data inform the scientific side, as shown by direct marketing, both traditional and digital. Creative executions and the strategic positioning behind them, brand stewardship and imaginative tactical executions inform the artistic side. The blend of the two seems to be the best of both worlds, and the exact ratio, the clinical recipe, varies with the company and the pre-set goals of the company.

Getting that mix "right" is what separates the rookies from the Most Valuable Players in marketing, and the best teacher is experience. Learning from others, however, even from their mistakes, can be important; hence this book. Failure is the fastest route to success in many cases, but doing all the necessary home-work, the due diligence, the research, is a great way to get a jumpstart on all that learning by doing. Learning from others' mistakes is an allowable shortcut to making good marketing decisions. That doesn't mean that reading every marketing book on the shelf (even this one), is going to put you ahead of the competition. There is no real substitute for grinding through the work of devis-ing the right research, finding the best list, testing creative concepts, reading the data, interpreting results, creating a budget and sticking to it, and all the other routine tasks a good marketer faces on a regular basis.

Marketing as an industry has created a specific language, including exclusive jargon, by which to communicate with others in the field. This language serves a few functions, including acting as a short-hand for insiders, making communication of routine details faster and more efficient for those in the know. It also creates a certain type of status through exclusivity. The thought being "If you don't' know what I'm talking about, you're not a true pro and have less knowledge than I do, and therefore can't criticize me," – it's a job security thing, like attorneys. And, like attorneys, it's also a little self-perpetuating, as the creative briefs, instructions to production resources, internal memos, briefings, and other communication ends up being rife with the stuff, and outsiders have trouble understanding it. Not really a good thing to deliberately create communication that obfuscates when our job entails creating clarity, but there it is.

There are any number of execution channels for marketing pros to bring to bear on the challenge of promoting, nurturing, marketing and raising awareness for their brand. Many of these are expounded upon in these pages, including public relations, advertising, direct mail, e-mail, trade shows, digital search engine, telemarketing, customer service, and social media. Each has an appropriate place in the mix, in the proper proportion, and as long as each is considered, and coordinated, to work with all the other selections, success is virtually inevitable. That level of integration is tough to achieve and one that is constantly sought as new tactics are discovered, invented or re-imagined. By allowing each media to show a common face to the customer, reinforcing the brand's attributes transparently and accurately, and for each to support the others both visually and functionally, marketers achieve real benefits, in terms of revenue and cost efficiency, and is therefore the Holy Grail for marketers.

Each channel has its own guidelines, its own pitfalls, its own set of generally accepted practices that help marketers who know and understand them avoid making what could be costly mistakes. However, for marketers, rules are made to be broken. In my practice, my company has had quite a few successes over the years that would seem to fly in the face of accepted wisdom. We can also point to a few instances where every rule and guideline was followed religiously and a miserable failure resulted. Most marketers' experiences fall somewhere in the middle most of the time, and the one's with the better batting average tend to rise to prominence. Unfortunately that prominence comes with a price tag, as the pressure to hit it out of the park as each new challenge presents itself builds, and expectations rise. Such success commoditizes the successes and magnifies the failures. That's where rules and guidelines can tip the odds in the marketer's favor, and that's why they're there – to codify the wins into some sort of replicable formula to reduce the likelihood of disaster.

The stories, recommendations, guidelines and suggestions in this book are intended to provide marketers with a framework, a skeleton, upon which to build their own experience library. They are based on over thirty years of experimental trial and error, of avoiding, bending, breaking, circumventing and twisting the accepted "rules" of marketing practice. The win/loss record in that time gives credence to the saying that rules were meant to be broken. There are many books on the marketing resource shelf written by highly-credentialed, highly-trained, scholarly academics that outline study after study, testing the rules over time, seeking best practice, showing the exceptions that prove the rules, and trying to explain the evolution of marketing practice in a codified way. This is not one of them.

Go forth and experiment . . .!

GLOSSARY

ASAE – American Society of Association Executives. The non-profit for employees of non-profits, and central depository of data and information, certification and best practices for the non-profit professional.

B-2-B – or B-to-B – Business To Business marketing, marketing activity that involve one business selling goods or services to another business as the end user, not to consumers or the end user.

Batch-and-Blast – marketing practice of sending out large volumes of e-mail at one time to an uncurated list.

Bouncebacks – term used to describe e-mail messages that do not reach the intended recipient.

Brick-and-Mortar – term referring to a real-world, physical building used to store and sell retail products, as opposed to an online product sales mechanism.

CSR – Customer Service Representative.

C-Suite, C-Level – Top management positions in a corporate structure – Chiefs of Finance, Operations, Information Technology, Marketing, and Executive Officer.

Emoticon – those nonsensical little symbols used to take the place of actual phrases in social media to save character count and time.

ISP – Internet Service Provider

Non-Dues Revenue – funds raised through the sale or licensing of intellectual property, copyrighted material or published information, conference attendance, educational seminars and any activity that is not covered by the annual dues fee in a non-profit organization.

NPO – non-profit organization, or not-for-profit organization, can be a charity, trade or professional association, hospital, or social services organization.

QA – Quality Assurance – a system of inspecting products or investigating the effectiveness of processes prior to them being delivered to the end user.

Recency – Direct Marketing term related to the age of a selected record's inclusion in a database selection, based on a purchase behavior. A person who bought from a catalog within the last 90 days would not be included in a list selection with a recency of 30 days or less.

ROI – Return on Investment - Marketing activity or any activity that more than covers the cost to implement.

SBA – Small Business Administration – Government entity chartered with fostering the growth and health of small business nationwide.

SEO – Search Engine Optimization. A technique used to make websites more prominent to search engine spiders by the use of keyword used most often to search for that product or service.

SPAM – term used to describe unwanted marketing e-mail from an unrecognized and unrequested source.

www.ingramcontent.com/pod-product-compliance
Lightning Source LLC
Chambersburg PA
CBHW071414170526
45165CB00001B/272

* 9 7 8 1 4 8 1 1 0 3 1 0 7 *